Sussex Cavalcade

by

Arthur R. Ankers

Revised and additional material

by

Michael Smith

Pond View Books

ISBN 1 871044 60 X

Printed in Great Britain by
Longmore Press Limited
Otford, Sevenoaks, Kent, TN14 5PG

Published by
Hawthorns Publications Limited
Pond View House, 6a High Street, Otford, Sevenoaks, Kent, England, TN14 5PQ

Sussex Cavalcade

Rev. Dr. Arthur R. Ankers, M.A., died on 18th August 1991. At his request the address at the
funeral service at Steyne Gardens Methodist Church, Worthing, included
the words of W.E. Henley, also for a time a Worthing resident,
as follows:

So be my passing!
My task accomplish'd and the long day done ...

CONTENTS

ERRATA
Illustrations
Page 83 Third picture - Bosham Creek and Holy Trinity Church
Page 95 The Church of St Andrew, Alfriston

Also by Arthur R Ankers

THE PATER

John Lockwood Kipling
His Life and Times
1837-1911

The Pater is the first ever biography of John Lockwood Kipling - and it is a story which deserves to be told. Quite apart from his influence upon, and his contributions to, his son Rudyard's work (for example, he illustrated *Kim* and *The Jungle Books*), he was, in his own right, a significant designer, journalist, author and teacher of arts and crafts.

" We should all consider ourselves indebted . . .
for this well-researched and enlightening book."

The Kipling Journal

ISBN 1 871044 00 6

Pond View Books

Dr. Ankers signing copies of *The Pater*, his biography of John Lockwood Kipling, at its launch at Bateman's on 14th June 1988.

LIST OF ILLUSTRATIONS

ACKNOWLEDGEMENTS

There can be few authors who, having completed a piece of work, are unaware of the fact that, in the words of Isaac Newton, they have 'stood on the shoulders of giants'. This has certainly been the case as I have striven to recover some of the rich tapestry of Sussex history and its association with Sussex places. I am especially indebted to E.V. Lucas and his *Highways and Byways in Sussex* and to David Harrison whose work, *Along the South Downs,* first fired my imagination when I came to live in Sussex. Also no student of Sussex history could fail to be grateful to that whimsical old Canon, Thomas Fuller who, in 1662, produced his *Worthies of England.*

I am further indebted to Rosalie Glynn Gryllis for her work on Edward Trelawny and Dante Gabriel Rossetti, and to John McGivering of the Kipling Society for his unfailing advice and encouragement. But this work could never have been completed without the patient help of those who, when I suffered a partial loss of eyesight, lent me their eyes. I refer to my friends Bill Riddell, Jack Humphrey, Clifford Pattison and Leon Strudwick who acted as research assistants and manuscript readers and, above all, to my wife Irene, without whose help the completion of the manuscript would have proved quite beyond me. Finally I am again indebted to Mrs. Margaret Littlewood who has been not only an amanuensis but also photographer and chauffeuse, enabling me to visit the places referred to in my work. Especially am I grateful to the present occupants of these places who have invariably received me with courtesy and helpfulness. Neither should I forget my teachers in bygone years who first inspired me with a love of history, nor the late Arthur Bryant whose historical works have captured the interest of many people in our island story.

Once again I am grateful to the staff of Worthing Central Library for their ready co-operation and help. To any who are deserving of mention but have been overlooked, I offer sincere apologies and my thanks, not least to the many authors of local histories and church guides whose researches have proved so helpful.

Arthur R. Ankers

I am indebted to T. Joe Smith of Rottingdean, a cricket historian, who kindly checked my material for Chapter V.

Michael Smith

Michael Smith has completely revised, and added new material to, Dr Ankers' original edition of *Sussex Cavalcade.* He has also added almost fifty of his own photographs to illustrate the text. A labour of love that has taken him all over Sussex.

In fact, Michael Smith served as a photographer with the Royal Air Force. After graduating from Reading University, he taught at a Royal Pakistan Air Force Cadet College, and at grammar and public schools before lecturing at Brighton College of Education. Whilst there, he established an exchange programme with universities in the US and was responsible for the Postgraduate Certificate of Education and for Teaching Studies. Now retired from teacher-training, he acts as a part-time lecturer for the Centre for Continuing Education of the University of Sussex.

He is the author of a number of textbooks, magazine articles, and modular learning programmes on geological and geographical topics, as well as several Ladybird Books for children. He has recently published a booklet, *Rudyard Kipling - The Rottingdean Years*, and was very much involved in the TVS television programme *Kipling's Sussex - A Fragile Paradise*.

Michael Smith travels extensively, giving lectures on all aspects of the geography and history of the county of Sussex, and on geological and geographical topics in general. All of which are illustrated with his own unique library of photographic slides.

He has served as Chairman of The Rottingdean Whiteway Centre, as Chairman of Governors of a local Primary School, and as Chairman of the Council of the Kipling Society, of which he is now the Honorary Secretary.

INTRODUCTION

When linked with people, places become alive. Similarly, ancient buildings can remain dead until they are inhabited, even if only through the imagination. Hence, the multiplicity of beds Elizabeth I is said to have slept in; the Sussex houses believed to have been given to Anne of Cleves as part of the price paid by Henry VIII to rid himself of his 'Flanders Mare'; the inns and great houses in which Charles II hid or found refreshment, while escaping from the Parliamentary forces after the disaster at Worcester in 1651. For like reasons, tourists flock to Stratford-upon-Avon - the birthplace of Shakespeare - and to the Lake District, where Wordsworth, Southey and Coleridge stayed and wrote.

Human interest is not only confined to people who were outstanding in English history and literature; it extends to half-forgotten people who made little or no impact on the course of history and yet whose lives and work were part of life's rich tapestry and may still be so, if only their 'simple annals' can be recovered. It was with this aim in mind that this book was written.

The county of Sussex is rich, not only in the number of ancient mansions, manors, churches and castles it possesses, but also in the variety of folk who have made their homes amid its Weald and Downs and beside its coast: soldiers and statesmen, poets and artists, manufacturers and inventors, sportsmen, pioneers and parsons. The list is endless.

There was a time when the Weald of Sussex was an important centre of industry, during which the great oak forests were denuded and the track-ways ruined as men mined and smelted and forged in pursuit of the business of iron- and glass-making. While great flocks of sheep grazed on the grassy Downs, below on the Weald men toiled in the manufacture, not only of household goods such as cooking utensils and fire-backs, but also of weapons of war, especially guns and armour, gunpowder and ammunition. Families with names such as Carryll, Gratwicke, Bowyer, Covert, Kempe and Shirley, whose memorials abound in the Sussex churches, were all involved to some degree in manufacturing. English-made cannon gained the reputation of being the best in the world and much of it was produced in Sussex.

By the late eighteenth century some of the roads, ruined by the heavy ox-drawn waggons which carried the ore and timber to furnace and forge, had been turnpiked and those who could afford it came to Sussex by private coach; others used the stagecoaches until their brief heyday was eclipsed by the advent of the railways. Some who ventured into Sussex as visitors stayed and became residents, buying land and building mansions and houses - great and small.

Not only did the county possess the advantages of lying along the South Coast and of being blessed with an equable climate with natural inland beauty, it was also not too distant from London. Thus it became possible for the more hardy of our ancestors to catch the early morning coach from Brighton to London, spend several hours on 'change' and be back home for supper. The age of the commuter had been born.

But it was the combination of peace and beauty, together with the fresh Channel breezes, which lured artists, poets and musicians to seek there the inspiration and quietness needed to pursue their art. They included people such as Alfred Lord Tennyson, William Blake, Edward Burne-Jones, Francis Thompson, Hilaire Belloc and, of course, Rudyard Kipling who, first at Rottingdean and then, for half his life, at Burwash, sang the praises of his adopted county, Sussex by the sea. Edward Elgar bought a remote cottage in the region of Fittleworth; John Ireland lived in a converted windmill near Washington; Hubert Parry lived at Rustington where he wrote the music to which Blake's *Jerusalem* was set.

Before the railways gave easy access to Sussex to the humbler part of the population, rich London merchants (and often rich lawyers) had bought or built their country homes within its boundaries. Having acquired the means, their ambition was to become men of property, and the possession of a place in the country became a status symbol. After buying a small country house and some thirty acres known as Bateman's, Kipling declared that he was now 'one of the gentry'! Long before Kipling, a timber-merchant, John Butler (who supplied some of the timber Samuel Pepys needed to rebuild the navies of Stuart kings) had built himself a lovely house in Burwash called Rampyndene. Before his time, a London mercer, Robert Palmer, had established himself near Angmering whilst Giles Garton, an ironmonger of the City of London, had built himself a house, in Armada year, on an estate he had bought at Woolavington. Its turbulent history of murder, deception and prophecy is still remembered locally. In the eighteenth century the house was reconstructed into an elegant mansion which is now the home of an independent school, Seaford College, set most snugly beneath the well-wooded scarp of the Downs beloved by Belloc.

Some older families, to whom these London merchants must have appeared as *nouveaux riches*, had long owned property in Sussex; others had received it at the time of the dissolution of the monasteries and other religious houses in the reign of Henry VIII. One such was Sir William Fitzwilliam, Earl of Southampton, who received Easebourne Priory in Midhurst. His successors also inherited the curse that went with the property - the great house, completed during the time of Sir Anthony Browne, first Lord Montagu, was destroyed by fire in September 1793. Although only a charred shell, it retains indications of its former splendour.

When the distribution of monastic lands put the Parham estate on the market, Robert Palmer snapped it up and, some years later, replaced the old house with the magnificent Elizabethan mansion which stands to this day.

Other people featured in the history of Sussex include the de la Warr family, whose ancestors fought at Poitiers and claimed to have captured King John of France (a boast disputed by the Pelham family) when the de la Warrs became the Sackville-Wests by marriage. Among those who have vanished into obscurity are the Shirleys from Wiston, whose great house remains and is used as a conference centre. Their ancestor, Sir Hugh, married an heiress of the de Braose and was killed in the Battle of Shrewsbury, in 1403. Nearly two hundred years later Sir Thomas Shirley, in debt, was forced to sell and the Shirleys sank into oblivion.

As well as Elizabethan mansions and houses of the aristocracy, Sussex abounds in more modest establishments, made famous by those who lived there. These include Victorian rectories, Edwardian guest houses, Georgian stately homes, even humble cottages and, of course, churches where the people worshipped and where their memorials are to be found. All these places can be brought to life by the discovery of who lived there, who went there, and what happened there.

It is over three hundred years since Dr. Thomas Fuller wrote in his *Worthies of England*: 'Many shires have done worthily, but Sussex surmounteth them all'. That was in 1662 and the men and women of Sussex who have followed have not proved unworthy of their heritage.

This book does not profess to be an academic history of the county. It is rather a collection of what might be called folklore, associated with a variety of buildings within its boundaries. Some of the stories related have a sound historical basis; others are tales which have accumulated through the years. To become a source of legend indicates something arresting in a person's character; witness: King Alfred and the cakes, Bruce and the spider, Walter Raleigh and his cloak, the Arthurian legends. These stories all involve people whose magnetism has attracted the anecdotes with which they have become associated. History would be less interesting without them.

Wiston House from the north-east, painted about 1640.
Reproduced by kind permission of Mr. R. H. Goring.

I   SEA-DOGS AND ADVENTURERS

Much has been written about the sea-dogs of Devon but little about their Sussex counterparts. Yet some of them fought side by side against the Spanish Armada and, like their fellow adventurers from Devon, sailed across the world, in search of either trade or plunder - preferably to be won at the expense of the hated Spanish, the Portuguese or the Dutch.

Among these sailor-families of Sussex were: the Shirley brothers from Wiston near Washington; the Palmers from New Place near Angmering, who later built Parham; the Coverts of Slaugham, one of whom had been involved in fortifying the Sussex coastline against the expected Spanish invasion - tried in 1588. Landings on the Sussex shore had been fully expected and Francis Drake had urged all Sussex landowners 'to look well to their coasts'. They responded by raising four thousand foot and two hundred and sixty horse, ready to repel the invaders.

The present mansion in Wiston Park was begun by Sir Thomas Shirley in 1574. During Queen Elizabeth's wars in the Netherlands, he had served as Treasurer-at-War, under the Earl of Leicester. Although the Queen had sought no territorial gains there, the fall of the great seaport of Antwerp to the Spanish had compelled her to send a force of five thousand foot and one thousand horse to help the Dutch resist the Duke of Parma.

In a day when corruption was rampant and it was regarded a military leader's privilege 'to feather his own nest', it is rather strange to find that Sir Thomas emerged from that campaign with 'small enrichment to himself'. Either he was uniquely honest or just incompetent for, on his return to England, he was alleged to be in debt to the Crown and was held in the Fleet prison. As he was Member of Parliament for Steyning, the eventual outcome of this unfortunate turn of events was a ruling by Parliament that its members should be secure from arrest, except for treason, felony or a breach of the peace. In this fashion Thomas Shirley (or Sherley) made history!

When Thomas Shirley of Wiston married Mistress Anne Kempe, daughter of a neighbouring landlord, Sir Thomas Kempe of Slindon Park, he joined an ancient family of Wye Manor, Kent. As part of her dowry, his bride brought with her several manors in Kent.

Mistress Kempe's ancestors had a distinguished record of service both to Church and State. For example, after holding several bishoprics, including Chichester and London, John Kempe, in the fifteenth century, was given the See of Canterbury and eventually became Lord Chancellor of England (it was said of him that he was more of a diplomat than a churchman). But he did found Wye College for the purpose of educating young men for the priesthood and was created a cardinal of the Roman Catholic Church.

Slindon Park, which was in the gift of the Crown, had formerly been occupied by Thomas Palmer, one of the famous Palmer triplets of New Place, Angmering. Not far away stood Petworth House, one of the seats of the Percy family, Earls of Northumberland. It was this family which conspired with the ailing King Edward VI, son of Henry VIII, to put Jane Grey, the daughter of the Protestant Earl of Dorset, on the throne rather than the rightful heir, Mary, daughter of Catherine of Aragon. The King, a bigoted Protestant, consented to the plot, while Northumberland sought to strengthen his own position by marrying his son Guildford Dudley to Lady Jane. He also involved several nobles in the conspiracy, as well as his neighbour at Slindon Park, Thomas Palmer.

Unfortunately for Northumberland the country could not stand by such an intrigue - East Anglia and the City of London stood firm for Mary Tudor and Northumberland had to surrender at Cambridge. Even a swift declaration of loyalty to Mary could not save him and his son who were both executed on Tower Green along with the tragic girl-Queen of nine days. Thomas Palmer shared the fate of his neighbours and, in 1554, the property at Slindon passed to the loyal Catholic family of Kempe.

It was Garret Kempe who, during the reign of Elizabeth, built the present mansion in Slindon Park. This is now the property of the National Trust and in use as a school. In the mid-sixteenth century it must have been a centre of plotting and high treason with the consequent arrest of the then owner and his henchmen, some of whom suffered a less dignified fate than their master. He was beheaded on Tower Green, but less important members of the plot were hung, drawn and quartered then hung in chains all around the City of London as a warning to others. It was a violent age and Sussex people, both Catholic and Protestant, found themselves among the victims.

According to a memorial once in Wiston church, the Lady Anne is described as Mistress Anne Kempe, daughter of Sir Thomas Kempe, 'with whom he (Thomas Shirley) lived in wedlock for ye space of fifty-three years. She bore him twelve children, five sons and seven daughters. Three of her children died in infancy, the residue being three sons and six daughters'. The monument was wantonly destroyed.

It was left to Thomas Shirley's three sons to seek to retrieve the family fortunes and, in so doing, they created one of the most extraordinary stories in English history.

The eldest of his three sons (also called Thomas) remained at home for a time, assisting his father with the management of their estate and the family's interests in the Sussex iron industry, viz. foundries which cast cannon. He, however, annoyed Queen Elizabeth by marrying one of her Maids of Honour, Frances Vavasour, without first seeking the royal permission. He was not alone in suffering royal disapproval for this type of offence; although Francis Walsingham was able to seduce one of the Queen's ladies and get away with it, others, who ventured on honourable matrimony, were not so fortunate. Walter Raleigh and Elizabeth Throckmorton had married without the Queen's permission and found themselves sent to the Tower to cool their ardour in separate rooms. Essex, the Queen's favourite, seduced several of her attendants without being punished simply by failing to marry any of them. When he married the widow of Sir Philip Sidney, however, Robert Devereux, Earl of Essex, was disgraced and banished from the Court.

After a temporary sojourn in prison, Thomas Shirley was set free and was, no doubt, glad to retreat into the rural fastnesses of Sussex, away from the royal wrath. But the gloomy financial situation he had inherited did not go away and in an attempt to improve it he decided to become a privateer.

The profession of privateering was not to be identified with that of piracy. In the eyes of the law, a pirate was a sea robber whose hand was against all men, whilst a privateer preyed only on his country's foes. He might even have been financed by a joint-stock company, set up for the purpose, and it was common belief that Her Majesty had had shares in the business; she was certainly not known to have refused a share in the loot! Nearly a hundred years later, Charles II was prepared to lend one of his ships for a similar enterprise, in this case against the Dutch.

Unfortunately, Thomas Shirley was not very successful in his new profession. Whilst prowling in the Mediterranean he was captured by the Ottoman Turks and, after two years in a Turkish jail, was released only through the personal intervention of King James I.

In order to protect naval secrets, a law was passed in 1574 which required all exporters of arms to be licensed. It seems that greed proved stronger than patriotism on the part of the gun-makers, for the Spanish fleet sailed against England armed, in part, with smuggled English cannon.

To smuggle cannon would seem to present special problems but one of the Shirley brothers, Robert, was reputed to have sold a gun to the Shah of Persia. (Perhaps it was part of the armament of his own ship.)

Anthony Shirley, brother to Thomas and Robert, went soldiering under the banner of Robert Devereux, Earl of Essex, who had persuaded the Queen to entrust him with a force sent to help Henry Navarre, the Protestant French monarch involved in a civil war against the Roman Catholic faction. Anthony had married a cousin of the Earl and was made one of his captains - an example, probably, of sixteenth-century nepotism.

The expedition was doomed from the start. The Queen had given Devereux permission to join it, against her better judgement. She lived to regret her weakness, for this gay, irresponsible young man soon demonstrated that her initial doubts were more than justified. He behaved with reckless bravado and achieved nothing. As a result he was ordered back to England, but before he obeyed, he added to his indiscretions by knighting twenty-four of his supporters. This folly only served to increase the royal anger: it cheapened an honour over which Elizabeth was inclined to be sensitive, but worse still, it would have constituted a sinister move on the part of Essex, for those who were so honoured were put in his debt and might subsequently be used as a threat to the State.

On his return from France, Anthony Shirley found himself in trouble for having accepted 'a French knighthood', possibly one of those conferred by Robert Devereux. Shirley escaped with a mild prison sentence. For a subsequent conspiracy against the Throne, Essex was sentenced to death.

On his release Anthony turned to seafaring, possibly feeling that 'life on the ocean wave' would be more comfortable than life at home in disgrace to his sovereign. On 21st May 1596, he sailed from Plymouth on the *Bevis*, accompanied by six smaller vessels. Arriving off the south-west African coast the expedition was met by 'a contagion of rain that did stink as it fell' - or so Thomas Fuller reported in his *Worthies of England*. Within six days conditions became unbearable so Anthony decided to sail westwards for the Caribbean. There he attacked Jamaica, then called St. Jago (as named by Columbus), and pillaged Spanish Town. Although his two hundred and eighty men were opposed by three thousand 'Portugals', he held the city for two days and nights before withdrawing. His voyage then took him to the Isle of Fuego where they were showered with ashes from a volcano. They were, however, able to obtain good water supplies before sailing for the island of Margarita. After further adventures, but now ill, short of food and deserted by his other ships, he set sail for England (via Newfoundland), arriving on 15th June 1597. In the view of Fuller this voyage, 'begun with more courage than counsel and pursued with more valour than advice, and gaining more honour than profit, is justly entitled to a prime place amongst the English adventurers'. By then Anthony had been at sea for just over a year.

The next voyage which the Shirley brothers, Anthony and Robert, made was of a different character and was to have both national and international significance. It is possible that they had come to the conclusion that the family fortunes were more likely to be restored by trading rather than by privateering, by commerce rather than by conquest. With this presumably in mind they headed for Aleppo in the Levant - the name given to the coastal regions of Syria and Asia Minor. The magnet which drew them could well have been the hostilities which had broken out between the Persians and their ancient foes, the Seljukian Turks. Given the Shirley family's involvement in the iron industry in Sussex - at the time reputed to make the best cannon in the world - a profitable intervention was no doubt in mind. Already a trading organisation, the Levant Company had bases at Smyrna and Aleppo.

On arrival they discovered that Shah Abbas was undecided about his future course of action. The Seljuks had been reinvigorated by their conversion to Islam and Persian morale was low because of the defeat of their troops to date. Anthony Shirley persuaded the reluctant Shah to continue the fight, whilst his brother, Robert, undertook to train the Persians and to instruct them in the use of artillery. This was supplied by the Shirleys, together with gunpowder and shot. Shah Abbas was attracted to these two young Sussex men: he appreciated their robust honesty and a quality of doggedness and reliability in them which compared favourably with the deviousness and corruption to be found in his Court. He created Anthony Shirley, Mirzah or Prince, and appointed him as his diplomatic representative to the Courts of Europe, being given the task of persuading European rulers to fight once more against 'the Infidel' or, at least, to apply 'economic sanctions' (as they would be called today) to Turkey.

Robert joined his brother in this ambassadorial role and visited the Pope, entering the Lateran Palace escorted by Swiss Guards. Not so successful were visits to Boris Gudenov, the Czar, and to Hampton Court, where King James I showed an interest in their suggestions but took no action. It was there that Robert came to blows with the Persian Ambassador and King James responded by packing both the combatants off to Persia to settle their differences at Isfahan. The Persian found himself in disgrace and committed suicide; Robert consequently felt he had been vindicated. In later travels he visited the Grand Mogul, the conqueror of India, at his Delhi palace.

In the military field he proved himself more successful. Like Henry Plantagenet, he employed his gift of rhetoric to raise the morale of his troops. A chronicler put these words in his mouth akin to those Shakespeare ascribed to Henry V: 'I will not encourage you with a long discourse for fear of putting oil on the flames, I should add spurs to a free horse. Your valiant resolution assures me that, were the enemy multitudes, and greater, yet with our quarrel good and our minds armed with true valour we shall return in triumph. Let me this day be the first in battle and be the last man on the field unless death give me an honourable quittance to my life. Let my actions be your precedent. Press as far as your General, courage gentleman, the victory is ours'! Then he fell so furiously on the enemy that the Turks were amazed at his valour.

The Turkish invasion penetrated as far as Vienna, having swallowed up Asia Minor, the Balkans, Hungary and reached the Calabrian district of Italy. There it failed to overrun the plains of central Europe and to subject all Christendom to the rule of Islam. Its arrest was due to the resistance of the Poles and Hungarians and the heroic defence of Malta by the Knights of St. John Hospitaller; but it is also true that the attacks by Robert Shirley's Persian force on the Turkish rear (not forgetting his guns) contributed to Europe's deliverance. True, their victory was only temporary, for the Seljuks were followed by a related tribe, the Ottoman Turks, who, under Suleiman the Magnificent, established an empire in the Middle East which continued until the end of the First World War.

Another and more lasting effect of the part played by the Shirley brothers was the establishment of British trading concerns in the Persian Gulf, especially the British East India Company.

At the entrance to the Gulf stood the fortress of Hormuz, occupied in the sixteenth and seventeenth centuries by the Portugese. In 1620 the Company's ships defeated a Portugese fleet; two years later, Robert Shirley led a combined force, supported by British ships, which captured Hormuz and expelled the 'Portugals'. This enabled the Company to build a factory which, in conjunction with one already established at Murut, Northwest India, gave 'John Company' a firm grasp on the lucrative trade in that part of the world. A new empire was in the course of being fashioned and two Sussex lads had a hand in it! Unhappily, the brothers quarrelled and Robert sought consolation for disappointment and homesickness in marriage. His bride was a seventeen-year-old Circassian girl named Teresia. She was the daughter of Ishmail Khan, a Christian and of noble birth, described as 'a duke of that country, a cousin-germane of the Shah being related to one of his wives'.

Teresia proved herself a true and helpful wife and travelled with Robert on his journeys. Like other Circassian girls, she was hardy as well as beautiful. She was with him when he died in 1628 and survived him by forty years.

During their travels in both Asia and Europe the Shirley brothers received many honours. In Prague, at the court of Rudolph II, Anthony was made a Count of the Holy Roman Empire, as was Robert. The Pope created Robert, Earle Knight of the Sacred Palace of Lateran with the privileges of the Knights of the Roman Empire and the Knights of Jerusalem. One such privilege was the power to legitimise bastards, but not those of 'great princes, earls and barons'.

After twelve years service abroad Robert returned to Wiston bringing his Circassian wife (now heavily pregnant) with him. He found his father broken in health and fortune and his brother, Thomas, in prison for debt. Teresia was most certainly the first Circassian lady to reach England, and as Robert delighted in wearing Persian costume, the two of them must have constituted a seven days' wonder as they walked the Sussex lanes. Robert, in fact, set an example to numbers of subsequent explorers by the wearing of what Fuller called 'foreign vestes'; it was a fashion to be followed by Lord Byron in Greece and both Wilfrid Blunt and T. E. Lawrence in Arabia. The portraits of Robert and his wife are to be seen at Petworth House. Fuller, commenting in his *Worthies of England*, thought that there was 'more ebony than ivory' in Teresia's complexion.

Detail of Wiston House.

Wiston at that time was probably near destitute of furnishings, Sir Thomas's goods having been seized by the Sheriff, so Robert wrote to Lord Salisbury on his father's behalf and the proceedings against Sir Thomas were stayed. Shortly afterwards Lady Teresia was delivered of a son. As Robert was in London at the time, his wife had the company of her mother-in-law, Lady Anne. Robert sought the consent of the Prince of Wales, Henry (elder brother of the future King Charles I), to sponsor the child, who was to be named after him. In the event the Queen acted as a godmother and the Prince of Wales as godfather. Unfortunately Prince Henry died the following year and Charles became King.

Robert's brother, Anthony, finding himself repudiated by his Queen owing to his lack of success in the Caribbean, took service with the Spanish in Morocco. He became Admiral of the Mediterranean Fleet, ending his life as a pensioner of Spain and, as some would have it, a traitor to his native land.

All these wanderings, fightings and adventurings did nothing to salvage the fortunes of the Shirley family, with the result that the eldest brother, Thomas, was compelled to sell his fair inheritance in Sussex. This he did to a neighbouring landowner, Sir John Fagge, who already held lands at Gratwicke and Aldbourne. A descendant, another Sir Robert, died without issue and bequeathed his property to his sister, Elizabeth. She married Sir Charles Matthew Goring and it was their son, Charles, who planted and nourished the beech trees which came to be known as Chanctonbury Ring, one of the best-known landmarks in the county. Sir John Fagge's portrait still hangs in Wiston but, when removed for cleaning, a large drawing was discovered on the wall where it had hung: the Forces' favourite during the Second World War, Jane, the pin-up girl (in reality a Horsham girl, Christine Drury). During the war the house had been requisitioned and the Canadian Saskatoon Light Infantry billeted there. Some unknown, but artistically gifted, Canadian soldier had left behind an amazing likeness of Jane, ten feet high, in the space left vacant when the famous portrait of Wiston's seventeenth-century owner had been taken down and stored for protection. Jane was to remain hidden and forgotten for more than forty years

This splendid mansion, and the adjoining church, are still to be seen; the house is used as a conference centre where leading figures in world affairs can meet and exchange views. The Foreign Office no longer has exclusive use of the property and its forty-eight bedrooms and fine public rooms are available for business conferences, private dinners and wedding receptions. Somehow one feels that the Shirley brothers would have approved the new venture: after all, in different ways they had all tried to salvage their lovely Sussex inheritance. Whilst they might well be mystified by the 'private facilities' which have been installed, they would probably recognise some of the cast-iron grates, the fire-backs and dogs, as being products of one of the family forges.

*　*　*　*　*

Another family of adventurers, destined to leave their mark on Sussex, was that of the Palmers. According to Thomas Fuller, their rise to prominence dates back to the landing of Henry Tudor at Milford Haven in 1485. He was welcomed there by one Clement, or Clemence, who supported him right up to the battle of Bosworth Field. He could even have been part of the conspiracy through which treachery decided the day so that five thousand rebels, marching under the Red Dragon of Cadwallader, as well as the standard of St. George, were able to defeat ten thousand soldiers commanded by King Richard III. One of Clemence's daughters married Edward Palmer and the family was rewarded with lands in Sussex. There, near Angmering, they built a house called New Place, now reduced to three cottages.

Mistress Palmer herself might have acquired a place in Sussex history: being two weeks in labour, she achieved what Fuller described as 'an act of superfoetation', by which he meant she gave birth to three sons on three successive Sundays, an achievement which E. V. Lucas believed to be 'well-attested'.

Not only were the Palmer sons to be remarkable for the circumstances of their birth, but all three, named Thomas, Henry and John, were to be knighted by Henry VIII, 'who never laid his sword on his shoulders who was not a man'. This was their reward for serving Henry in his wars against the strongest power in Europe at the time - France. Having allied himself with Spain, through marriage with Catherine of Aragon, Henry landed in person in the North of France and in 1514, aided by Austrian mercenaries, won the Battle of the Spurs, capturing Bayard, the most famous knight in Europe. The might of France was broken and England established once more as a power in Europe.

12

It was only the treachery of his Spanish allies which prevented him from recovering 'his heritage of France'.

Henry Palmer served as a soldier at Boulogne and Calais but at the fall of Calais, when England lost her last foothold on the continent, Henry was taken prisoner. He was ransomed and died in the first year of the reign of Elizabeth, 1559.

Thomas Palmer, described as a soldier of great courage, was unable to keep away from conspiracies, a weakness which led to his undoing. He conspired with 'Protector Somerset' in a treasonable plot but, according to Fuller, turned 'super-grass' and through this act of treachery to his associates, saved his own skin - for a time. As already related, he joined in another conspiracy which aimed at denying the throne to Mary Tudor and giving it to seventeen-year-old Lady Jane Grey. This time Palmer did not escape royal retribution and lost his head on the block.

The third son of Edward Palmer, John, became High Sheriff of Surrey and subsequently of Sussex. He was a notorious gambler and won money from King Henry at cards. Henry was a bad loser and could never forgive Francis I of France for defeating him at wrestling at 'the Field of Cloth of Gold'. It seems that John Palmer had also managed to affront the royal self-respect, for, in Fuller's words, 'he was hanged, on what grounds it is not known'.

Perhaps it was because Henry never liked losing!

Another member of the Palmer family had chosen a safer and more rewarding way to affluence. He had set himself up as a mercer in the City of London and must have prospered because, in 1577, his great-grandson, also called Thomas, laid the foundation stone of a splendid new mansion known as Parham.

Before the new Parham was built, a thatched hall stood on the site. It had belonged to the Abbot of Westminster although the Palmers had leased it. At the time of the dissolution of the monasteries they bought it and some of the building materials from the old house were then used in the construction of the new one.

Thomas Palmer, who laid the Parham foundation stone, was seized with the adventurous spirit of his ancestors. He served under Drake and Hawkins and in the foray which Walter Raleigh led against the Spaniards in 1596. He so distinguished himself in that engagement that he was knighted aboard the Lord-Admiral's ship. He had shared in the destruction of thirteen Spanish vessels and a vast quantity of stores, thus averting a repetition of Philip of Spain's 'Enterprise England', eight years earlier. It was said that the Lord-Admiral, Thomas Howard, 'made many knights on that occasion, almost all that did deserve it'!

Another member of this famous family, Sir Henry Palmer, son of Thomas, served, as a young man, under Lord Howard of Effingham and Sir Francis Drake as they awaited the Armada's progress up the Channel. He was a member of the Eastern Squadron whose job it was to keep watch on the ports of Dunkerque and Sluys in order to prevent the Duke of Parma from making a landing on the English shore.

The Eastern Squadron was commanded by Sir William Wynter and, when the Armada cast anchor off Calais, it was plain to him that if they were to be moved, it would only be by the employment of fire-ships. Accordingly, he dispatched Henry Palmer in a pinnace to Dover where Walsingham had fishing boats, loaded with faggots and pitch, ready for such an emergency.

But when Drake arrived on the scene, he saw that there was no time to be lost; both wind and tide were favourable for the undertaking. Drake offered one of his own vessels to be used as a fire-ship. Hawkins, not to be outdone, offered one of his, and four others did likewise. The six ships thus provided were packed with any combustible material that could be found and, with full sails set and blazing, they bore down upon the enemy. Loaded cannon had been left aboard, and these exploded when the heat of the fire reached them. Believing that they were being attacked by hell-burners (a kind of floating bomb), capable of killing more men in one blast than might fall in a great battle, the Spaniards panicked, cut their anchors and headed for the open North Sea. There the waiting English were able to engage them and chase them northwards. It is easy to imagine the disappointment of Henry Palmer when, on his return, he found that his squadron had vanished and he had been denied participation of what was to be hailed as a famous victory. Such are the fortunes of war!

The end of the Palmer story is a sad one. Sir Thomas, following his exploits at Cadiz in 1596, returned to Parham, fell out with his wife and, twenty-five years after its completion, let the house to Thomas Byshopp, a lawyer from Henfield. Sir Thomas then retired to Spain, only to die of smallpox in 1605 - a miserable end to the Wiston branch of a famous Sussex family. But Parham still stands, a monument to a bygone age and a joy to the present one. It is open regularly to the public though it is retained in private ownership.

* * * * *

One who had his full share of adventure, in the service of his Sovereign, was George Augustus Eliott. During the Seven Years War (1756-1763) fought mainly against the French, England sought to protect her colonial interests. At this time, General George Eliott was second-in-command at the capture of Havana, Cuba, in the Caribbean. He used his share of the prize money to buy an estate at Heathfield. A few years later, his renowned asceticism stood him in good stead during the protracted siege of Gibraltar. Again the Spaniards were the enemy.

The Moors had used the Rock, one of the ancient Pillars of Hercules, as a natural defence since early in the eighth century. The Spaniards first gained control in 1309 but lost it again until 1462 when they made it all but impregnable. However, during the War of Spanish Succession a combined British and Dutch force captured it after only a three day siege and possession was taken in the name of Queen Anne. Repeated Spanish endeavours to recapture the Rock failed and after a few years attempts stopped.

It was not until 1779, during the American War of Independence, that Spain, once more, tried to wrest it back. A monumental siege of three and a half years duration brought great privation to the beleaguered garrison under the command of General Eliott, in spite of occasional re-victualling by the Royal Navy. Relief was finally achieved following a naval victory of Admiral Howe in 1783. Later in the same year a formal peace was concluded between England, France, Spain and Holland at the Treaty of Versailles, and British sovereignty of the Rock was confirmed in exchange for return of Minorca to the Spaniards and Tobago to the French. Sir George's personal stoicism in such near famine conditions inspired his men. His Knighthood was followed by ennoblement as Baron Heathfield of Gibraltar.

Although Lord Heathfield spent relatively little time at his Sussex estate (up until his death in 1790), the subsequent owner, Sir Francis Newberry, had a tower folly built in the park to celebrate his achievement. In it he assembled a number of Lord Heathfield's personal effects, including some which had been with him during the siege. These, sadly, were later dispersed. Damaged by fire during the Second World War, the tower was restored by Dr Gerald Moore in 1968 to house a military museum.

Brede Place in 1858.
Reproduced by kind permission of Mr. Jonathan Frewen.

II   MORE ADVENTURERS OF A DIFFERENT KIND

The Sussex coast was destined to become a favourite goal for those who sought retirement from the heat and burden of life's day. None was more remarkable than Edward John Trelawny who retired to Sompting towards the end of a startlingly colourful life.

He was not a son of Sussex, being born into a distinguished Cornish family. One of his ancestors had been a bishop but few vestiges of his Christian inheritance were to appear in Edward's career, though some may be seen in aspects of his character, for he was a strange amalgam of vice and virtue.

Born in the closing years of the eighteenth century, he suffered much cruelty at the hands of a tyrannical father and a loving, though rather intimidating, mother. It is not known which school he attended (his father had been at Westminster but objected to the expense on behalf of his son). What is known is that Edward became a holy terror to the staff on account of both his stature and temper. He plotted with other boys to give one of the unpopular teachers the kind of flogging he usually handed out to his pupils. When confronted by the Head, Trelawny seems to have seized the reverend gentleman in a kind of rugby tackle so that he banged the back of his head on the floor. Confined to a cold room, he set the curtains of the bed on fire. Not surprisingly, he was expelled. When he arrived home his father made no comment, being glad to be relieved of school fees. Instead, rather than settle his younger son in one of the family 'livings', which usually followed a season at Oxford, the boy, whilst scarcely thirteen years old, was sent to sea as a cadet. The year was 1805, the year of Trafalgar and the death of Nelson.

He was sent to join Nelson's squadron but it seems that his captain was not over eager to join the fight and the ship put into Plymouth for mutton and potatoes. It missed the great sea fight by two days. With Edward paid off on his ship's return to port, his father directed that he should be taken to Dr. Burney's School of Navigation at Gosport and it was there that his serious sea training began.

His first voyage as one of His Majesty's sea cadets took him to Bombay, by which time he had discovered that life on board, though more tolerable than life at school, was a little worse than life at home, so he deserted.

He had made contact in Bombay with a man who called himself de Ruyter but whose real name was the humbler de Witt. He was a privateer who, despite his name, sometimes flew the French flag and was happy to appoint the trained young navigator to command one of his ships. The offer was too good to miss, Trelawny had already nearly murdered a Scots naval lieutenant who was persecuting one of his fellow cadets, Walter Aston, so it was in his best interests to dispose of his naval uniform, with its white facings on blue cloth, and to adopt the garb of an Arab corsair.

At one time de Ruyter was called on by a French warship to help expel some Mahratti pirates who had landed on Madagascar and were creating mayhem among the inhabitants. In the course of the fight which followed, Trelawny rescued the daughter of an old Sheik killed by the pirates and brought her back to the ship. As her father lay dying he had pressed a ring on Trelawny's finger and joined his hand with that of his daughter, supposedly a form of marriage. Her name was Zella and Edward called her his 'little orphan bride'. 'Our happiness', he wrote, 'could admit of no augmentation; it was perfect'. Not only was Zella beautiful but she was brave, and twice saved her husband's life. On one occasion he was wounded in the groin and for months she nursed him, applying native treatments of raw egg applications and herbs; also she refused to let the ship's surgeon bleed him. When the ship was overwhelmed by a sudden storm and Edward was in danger of drowning, it was Zella, though pregnant, who threw him a rope; as a result she suffered a miscarriage.

Shortly afterwards, whilst sailing near Java, Edward was 'fancied' by a monstrous Javanese widow. He repelled her and she revenged herself by sending a servant to Zella with some poisoned sweets: a few hours afterwards Zella died in agony. 'With her lips pressed towards mine', he wrote, 'she yielded up her mortality'. Something in Trelawny died with Zella.

He gave up privateering and returned to Regency England where, in his words, 'The fatal noose was cast round my neck; the bloody bit thrust into my mouth'. He married Caroline Julia Anderson when he was scarcely twenty-one.

His heart cannot have been in this matter for it was not long before his wife found a lover in the form of a Captain Colman. Her husband discovered their liaison and left her. He commenced divorce proceedings, a cumbersome undertaking in those days, and it was not until 1819 that he found himself a free man.

After the stirring events of the previous years, Trelawny found life dull and stale. He sought solace in literature, delighted in Shakespeare and, before Wordsworth was widely recognised, discovered that behind the hard features and weather-stained brow there was 'a divinity within'.

It was while in Switzerland in 1820 that he discovered the genius of Percy Bysshe Shelley. During that visit he also met Wordsworth and his sister and heard him protesting about the wretches who had cut roads through the Alps and the Appenines, thus opening up the mountains to carriages. Trelawny asked Wordsworth what he thought of Shelley as a poet and received the abrupt answer, 'Nothing'. He also observed with amusement how the English thawed rapidly when they drifted into a warmer climate; possibly he had in mind Wordsworth and his liaison with Annette Vallon. (The relationship had begun in Orleans and resulted in the birth of a girl.)

It was through what Trelawny often referred to as 'a touch of fate' that he met Shelley and became a member of his coterie. Meeting with Thomas Medwin and Edward Williams (with whom he was already acquainted), he was introduced to Shelley. He also met Mary, Shelley's wife, whom he described as 'slim, very fair, with wide grey eyes ... the brilliant author of *Frankenstein*'. To her, he appeared like a noble pirate - the nearest she had ever come to; a kind of half-Arab-Englishman. Shelley wrote of Trelawny: 'He was as the sun in his first youth, beautiful and terrible as a tempest'.

Trelawny also met Byron, to whom he seemed the personification of a corsair, but Trelawny was disappointed in Byron - 'jealous and impulsive as a woman and maybe as changeable'. But later, after Byron died, he wrote: 'With all his faults I loved him truly. He is connected with every event of the most interesting years of my wandering life'. Byron said that if only they could persuade Trelawny to wash his hands and not tell lies, he would be a gentleman. Also in this party was Claire Clermont, with whom Byron had been involved. For his part, Trelawny was more attracted to Mary Shelley, the daughter of Mary Wollstonecraft, and, in a weak moment, treated her 'with something like impertinence', according to her account. Mary may well have led him on for she described him, glowingly, as being 'six feet tall with raven-black hair and short thick curls, dark grey expressive eyes, upturned lips and a smile which expressed good nature and kind-heartedness'. She could hardly have remained indifferent to such a paragon! In any case, Shelley himself admitted that he and his wife were an ill-matched pair. 'Poor Mary', he said, 'hers is a sad fate. She can't bear solitude, nor I society - the quick coupled with the dead'.

Shelley and his friends now decided to look for two villas on the Italian Riviera. He also consulted with Trelawny about a boat he was having built at Genoa. Edward told him that, as he neither smoked nor drank alcohol, he would never make a sailor. Nevertheless, he pressed on with his project. His craft was to be named Don Juan, a tribute to Byron who was also having a schooner built - to be named *Bolivar*.

Whilst the two boats were under construction, Shelley and his friend Edward Williams hunted along the coast for two suitable homes, but in vain. In the end they settled on sharing a former Jesuit convent, Casa Magni, which stood close to the shore with a verandah overhanging the waves. Unfortunately this meant that the unpaved ground floor was uninhabitable because, in stormy weather, the sea used to invade it. Shelley was charmed with the solitude of the place, with the sea in front and the dark woods behind.

On 8th July 1822 Trelawny and Shelley arrived at Leghorn where, in the harbour, Edward Williams, the co-owner of Shelley's boat, awaited them together with the boat-boy, Charles Vivian. Shelley had renamed his boat *Ariel*, and he and Williams proposed to sail to Casa Magni that same day. Trelawny, the professional sailor, had less confidence in the new owners' seamanship than they possessed themselves and proposed to escort them to Spezzia in his new ship, *Bolivar*. Unhappily, the port authorities refused to grant him clearance, with the result that Shelley and Williams set sail without him.

It was a blisteringly hot summer's afternoon. Though warned of a prospective storm, the two novice sailors and the boat-boy set out. Trelawny, with a heavy heart, watched them go.

Shelley had arranged for his boat to be designed more with an eye to beauty than seaworthiness. She had lovely sweeping lines but needed over two tons of ballast to make her sailable in any but the calmest of seas. Her crew were never seen alive again.

Trelawny offered a substantial reward for the recovery of his friends' bodies. After about a week, Shelley's was washed ashore; later, they found Williams and all that remained of the ship's boy after sea creatures had done with him. Shelley's body was badly mutilated; the boy's was little more than a skeleton.

The sanitary laws demanded that the bodies be burned on the beach and Trelawny undertook the melancholy and rather gruesome task. After three hours of incineration, Byron could no longer bear the sight, and plunging into the sea, swam out to the *Bolivar*. Trelawny snatched Shelley's heart from the flames and severely burnt his hand in the process. Shelley had always hoped to be buried in the Protestant Cemetery in Rome where John Keats was buried, and they carried out his wishes.

Following the death of Shelley and his companions, Casa Magni was given up and Mary Shelley and Jane Williams returned to England. Some months later, in a fit of chivalry, Trelawny offered to marry Mary, but she turned him down saying that Mary Shelley was such a pretty name she did not wish to change it.

Trelawny and Byron then went to Genoa to meet a Captain Blanquiere who represented the Anglo-Greek Committee for Greek Liberation. Trelawny had indicated to the captain Lord Byron's interest and concern regarding the struggle of the Greek people against their oppressors, the Turks, and the terrible defeat they had already suffered in 1821.

After negotiations, Byron chartered a ship, the *Hercules*, and in company with Trelawny and ten thousand pounds sterling, sailed for Greece. Trelawny could never resist a fight, especially when it was on the side of a small nation subjugated by a bigger one. They landed at the coastal town of Missolonghi.

As his physical limitations prevented Byron from taking a soldier's part in the struggle, he stayed down on the coast in order to confer with the Greeks and to raise funds for their support. It was January 1824 and a miserable winter, during which he caught a fever. In accordance with prevailing medical fashions he was mercilessly bled by the doctors, and on 19th April 1824, he died. Within the space of two years Trelawny had been bereft of both his friends.

The bitterness of his loss was increased by the knowledge that, had he been present, he might have saved them both. If only he had sailed in company with Shelley on that last fatal voyage, the poet might well have been rescued. Trelawny was a very strong swimmer who had swum the Hellespont (a feat of which he was proud) and had even tackled the Niagara River, though unsuccessfully. Again, if only he had remained in the company of Byron he would certainly have prevented the doctors from bleeding him to death, just as he was to refuse their attentions when he himself was wounded. But Trelawny, never one to absent himself when a fight was promised, was away in a cave fortress on Parnassos, fighting with one of the Greek resistance leaders called Odysseus.

While living in this immense natural fortress, Trelawny married the sister of Odysseus, a mere child named Tersitza. She bore him a child who was christened Zella - the name of the Arab girl he had rescued in Madagascar and who had, on two occasions, saved his life. Trelawny also took to wearing Greek dress, the costume in which he was to be painted by Seymour Kirkup but, when his young wife managed to procure a fashionable dress from Paris, he punished her by cutting off her hair with his dagger. He disliked the female frame boned by stays into an unnatural shape and surmounted by fantastic millinery. With wifely submission, Tersitza neither wept nor grumbled: she simply left him and took refuge in a convent. When her second child was born she sent the babe to its father. He put it out to nurse but the poor little thing died. Then Trelawny had the tiny corpse put in a box and posted back to its mother. Certainly he was a grim and savage man in some ways; in others, kind, thoughtful and compassionate.

Trelawny's return to England was precipitated by an incident which nearly cost him his life. A spy had infiltrated the fortress on Parnassos and shot him in the back. Remembering the treatment prescribed by his Arab 'wife', Zella, he refused to be bled by the doctors and insisted that his wounds be treated with the white of egg and exposure to the sun. After a long illness he found that his wounds had left him *hors de combat* and so he arranged for a British ship to transport him back to England.

Reaching London, he quickly found himself being lionised on account of his associations with Shelley and Byron. He also found that Byron's death had done more for Greek independence than he had ever managed to do during his lifetime. The shock of his death was such that in 1827 an alliance of British, French and Russian ships was mobilised and defeated the Turkish and Egyptian fleets in the Battle of Navarino.

Following his return, Trelawny met a Sussex Lady, Augusta Goring, wife of Sir Harry Goring. They lived together and the ensuing divorce proved to be a *cause célèbre*. He took a farm near Usk where he and Augusta lived for twenty years and brought up a family. Then they separated, but since a daughter, Laetitia, went to live with Trelawny for a time, it is supposed that she felt that the blame for the breakdown of the relationship was not her father's.

In 1870 an odd train of circumstances brought this former sailor, privateer and soldier of fortune to a peaceful retirement in the village of Sompting, two miles from Worthing, Sussex.

He numbered among his London friends, William Rossetti, a younger brother of the famous artist-poet, and son of an Italian patriot in exile, Gabriel Rossetti. William had sent Trelawny a present of some green figs. He so enjoyed them that he thought of buying the tree. This grew in the garden of a cottage in Sompting but, on arriving there, he found the owner unwilling to sell. In order to gain possession of the tree he bought the cottage as well and retired there.

For a time his daughter lived with him but he also gained a companion in Miss J. Taylor, believed by the locals to be his housekeeper 'and something more'. (His track record would suggest that this was not unlikely.)

The new resident soon gained the reputation of being a fiery old man! On one occasion a local bully stuck his wife in the copper and, when Trelawny heard of it, he went to the house, rescued the wife and replaced her in the copper with her husband - a proceeding hardly calculated to restore domestic bliss, one would think.

Every day, winter and summer alike, he could be seen riding down to the beach for a swim or walking to the local pond to feed the ducks. He always had a supply of Turkish delight to give to children he met on the way. His garden became a bird sanctuary and he taught the birds to come for crumbs when he rang a bell. Rumour had it that, meeting a neighbour one Sunday morn, he demanded if she went to church. When she replied 'No', he seized her by the arm and propelled her into the parish church saying 'There is time for you to start!'.

This strangely complex character had abandoned what he called his 'grog' and, when J. F. Watts painted him with a glass at his elbow, he rounded on the artist. He also rid himself of his sporting gun.

In the end Trelawny died a peaceful death in Sompting but not before he had arranged with the custodian of the Protestant Cemetery in Rome to be buried there; his grave to be covered by a stone bearing Shelley's words:

Here lie two friends whose lives were undivided,
Let not their bones be parted for their two hearts,
In life, were single-hearted.

The cottage which bears his name, is still to be seen in Sompting, close to the Gardeners Arms.

Edward Trelawny was not to be the only adventurer who sought a peaceful retirement in Sussex - another was Colonel Henry Wemyss Feilden.

He was the son of John Leyland Feilden who had married a Miss Wemyss and lived at Feniscowles near Blackburn, Lancashire. After school at St. Andrews and Cheltenham, Henry was commissioned in the 42nd Regiment of Foot, the Black Watch, a Scottish regiment so called on account of the dark tartan which was part of their uniform. He served with his regiment during the Indian Mutiny, was present at the Relief of Lucknow and, subsequently, saw service in China, following the Taiping Rebellion.

Still only twenty-one years of age he resigned his commission and, with one thousand pounds (gained it was said through racing horses and from loot following the events at Lucknow), he sailed for North America. The three ships which constituted his expedition were loaded with articles in short supply among the Southern Confederates - blankets and other basic necessities. Having evaded a Yankee frigate by dodging into a fog belt, the little fleet made landfall off Charleston, Virginia.

By nature Henry Feilden was not cut out to be a 'box-wallah' (the Anglo-Indian name for a street-trader or for anyone associated with trade). At heart he was a soldier and, like Trelawny, a man of action. Thus, it is not surprising to find that he was soon fighting on the side of the Confederates. When General Robert E. Lee finally surrendered at Richmond, Virginia, Feilden was among his *aides-de-camp*. He left a vivid description of the plight of the Southern forces at the time of the surrender. 'We had finished robbing the grave and begun on the cradle', he wrote, and described how, during the last months of the war between the states, he had served in company with fifteen thousand boys of under seventeen years of age without seeing one of them smile.

During his service with the Confederates, Feilden had married. His bride was Julia McCord, daughter of Judge David McCord and, because there was very little gold in Richmond, Feilden had the wedding ring made out of a gold sovereign.

After the war he returned to England, bringing his bride with him. It was the year 1866 and he was fortunate enough to secure the appointment of Paymaster to the 18th Hussars with whom he saw service in India.

But Henry Feilden had other gifts as well as that of soldiering: he was an accomplished botanist and naturalist. It was in this capacity that he was invited to accompany the Arctic expedition under command of Sir George Strong Nares. The expedition which consisted of two ships, HMS *Alert* and

Discovery, spent the winter of 1879-1880 off Ellesmere Island and, for his scientific work, Feilden was awarded the coveted Polar Medal.

About ten years after the Arctic adventure, Colonel Feilden travelled to Natal where his family had interests. While there, he learned of the birth of the first European baby to be born on the edge of Zululand, so he and a friend rode twenty-seven miles to meet the family. In this way he met Henry Rider Haggard, the famous novelist, who enchanted England with his tales of high adventure in the 'dark continent'. Haggard had resigned his legal post in Pretoria and taken up ostrich-farming, at a time when the feathers of these splendid birds were much in demand by the fashion houses of Europe. The baby was Rider Haggard's son, always known as Jock, though baptised Arthur. Haggard and Colonel Feilden were to meet again at Bateman's, near Burwash, Sussex.

It was in 1902 that the Feildens came to live at Burwash. In the same year Rudyard Kipling had bought Bateman's and moved there from Rottingdean. Both the Feildens and the Kiplings stayed at the Bear, Burwash, whilst their new homes were being made ready for them, and a friendship was begun which lasted until Feilden's death in 1922.

Rampyndene, Burwash.

Rampyndene, the Burwash house to which the Feildens came in 1902, was a lovely William and Mary house, built by John Butler who, in the days when Samuel Pepys was building the navy for Charles II and his brother James, had supplied oak timber from the Weald with which to build 'Hearts of Oak'. It was at a time when the Navy suffered sadly through corruption and incompetence and which gave Pepys the chance to earn, through his energy and abilities, the title of 'the Saviour of the Navy'. The house that Butler built, with its high roof, its tall chimneys and its lovely shell-like porch, is still one of the jewels in the main street of Burwash.

Colonel Feilden became a father figure to Kipling. He gave guidance regarding estate management to this novice among landowners. He showed him how to stock the Dudwell river with trout - and how to catch them. He even proffered guidance on the subject of speech-making. When Rudyard was due in Edinburgh to receive an honorary doctorate from the Scottish university, his friend advised him to 'avoid prolixity and the Scottish accent'. The advice must have been taken for it seems that the speech was well received.

Although Feilden was twenty-six years senior to Kipling, his death on 18th June 1922 came as a severe blow. Despite his eighty-two years he had been able to walk Rudyard 'off his feet and bring down pheasants from high heaven' - being a strong walker and expert shot. Yet by nature he was (according to Kipling) 'as shy and diffident as an old maid'. Judged by Kipling's own standards he was also a true man.

* * * * *

The third of this trio of latter-day adventurers was Moreton Frewen, in many ways a contrast to Trelawny and Feilden, in others, sharing several of their characteristics.

He was born at a house called Brickwall in the Sussex village of Northiam. The Frewens had long lived there and some of his forebears had distinguished themselves in the course of English history. When Queen Elizabeth visited Northiam they were among those who waited on her as she dined under the trees on the village green. Other members of the family had gone into exile rather than surrender their Puritan principles.

Born in 1853, Moreton was the Frewen's third son. He came to be known not just as Moreton Frewen, but also as 'Mortal Ruin'; this on account of his financial adventures which proved costly to those of his friends who shared his losses.

In his youth, Moreton had been a first-class shot - one of the best in England and thus when, in 1915, aged sixty-two, H.M. Government refused him permission to go out to France 'to shoot Germans', he was greatly grieved. He was also a handsome 'man-about-town' and much in demand at country house-parties.

It was in the 1870's that Moreton sailed for the United States of America in search of a fortune. He took with him sixteen thousand pounds and, on his return some years later, he had debts to the tune of thirty thousand!

In the States he bought land on the banks of the Powder River, Wyoming, and set himself up as a cattle-rancher. A huge log-house was built, grandiloquently named Frewen Castle, and soon Moreton was a member of the famous Cheyenne Club and a cattle baron. During the last quarter of the nineteenth century this coterie virtually ruled Wyoming.

It was also at a time when the great herds of bison which had roamed the prairies were near extinction, yielding up their ancient feeding grounds to the farmer and rancher. Not only did Frewen invest his own money in the new enterprise, he also persuaded friends, including Lord Lonsdale and Lord Dunraven, to do the same. But his enterprise encountered difficult days: blizzards, droughts and over-grazing, combined with inexperience, led to ruin.

Short of money, Moreton had the sense 'to go where money is'; in other words to New York where, in a brownstone mansion in Madison Square, he met one of the daughters of the wealthy banker, Leonard Jerome. Another of Jerome's daughters, Jeanette, was already married to Lord Randolph Churchill and Mrs Jerome rather fancied a duke for Clara, her second daughter. But when Clara set eyes on the tall, dark Englishman, all thoughts of a title evaporated. She and Moreton married in Grace Church and departed to spend their honeymoon on Outfit 76, along the Powder River, Wyoming.

They travelled by rail to the railhead, ninety miles from Frewen Castle, there to be met by a hundred cowboys who had come to welcome the boss and his lady and to escort their coach to their home. On arrival, some of the cowboys serenaded the newly-weds from the minstrels' gallery, built into the dining hall of the 'castle'; Clara was charmed.

In the years to come it may well have been that she had second thoughts about marrying in haste, as Moreton proved to be a difficult husband and was frequently unfaithful. Among his conquests was the actress, Lily Langtry. He tried to teach her to ride but every time the horse began to move she shrieked. At last he found her a reliable mount called Redskin on which she managed a sedate progress along Rotten Row. It was there that King Edward VII saw and admired her; from then on an impoverished cattle-baron had no chance against a crowned head.

In 1896 fate came to the rescue of Moreton's precarious financial circumstances: an uncle drowned whilst sailing and Moreton found himself the owner of a property on the banks of the River Bandon, County Cork. It was a shooting lodge called Innishannon and there, his children, Clare and Oswald, found an exciting new world to explore. Moreton was even elected M.P. for North-East Cork and held his seat from 1911 to 1914. He then resigned in favour of Tim Heeley. Unfortunately, during 'the Troubles' (as the Irish came to call them) Innishannon was burned down, a fate shared by five of Frewen's neighbours. His Scots gamekeeper was murdered and the hatchery, his pride and joy, destroyed - as were the spawn of trout and salmon it contained. This bitter blow was made still more bitter by the fact that, politically, Moreton was a Home Ruler and had a deep concern for the plight of the Irish rural poor.

Back in England, the Frewens had been given Brede Place, on the Brickwall Estate, a fourteenth-century house which had been enlarged in the sixteenth century. It stood on a ledge overlooking the Brede River and was believed to be the oldest inhabited house in England after Windsor Castle. It certainly looked it when Moreton took possession. It had long been neglected and was nearly derelict; most of the floors and window panes were non-existent and the chapel had been used as a storehouse for grain and straw. But Clara loved it, especially the east window which remained intact. She determined to restore the old house, which she did during intervals between periods of their insolvency.

The Moreton Frewens were 'given to hospitality' and many leading figures, especially in the field of literature, seem to have gravitated there: Henry James often cycled over from nearby Rye; Joseph Conrad came from Ashford; H. G. Wells from Folkestone and, of course, the Kiplings from Burwash.

At first the house had no electric light or adequate heating and the sanitation was medieval. This consisted of earth closets, sixteen of them, half-way up a hill so that when H. G. Wells stayed overnight, following a house-party, he grumbled that, with the coming of daylight he looked out on a wintry landscape 'studded with melancholy, preoccupied, male guests'.

In 1897, Moreton's nephew, Winston Spencer Churchill, had gone to India and was writing his *Malakand Field Force*. In order to save time he entrusted the correction of his proofs to his Uncle Frewen, described by him as a brilliant man and a ready reader. Moreton substituted some of the rolling Churchillian phrases, reminiscent of Gibbon, with plain and simple prose. Unfortunately, he was not a good proof-reader and the first edition appeared with 'many scores of shocking misprints and with no attempt to organise the punctuation', or so Winston complained. But after sarcastic comments on the misprints, the critics vied with one another in its praise. Moreton also obtained for Winston, the aspiring journalist, his first typewriter and persuaded the Duchess of Marlborough to pay for it!

He had long been an admirer of the young Kipling and had sent some of the *Barrack Room Ballads* to *The Daily Telegraph*, only to have them returned as not up to the newspaper's standards.

In 1903, Buffalo Bill's Wild West Show was performing at Earls Court and Morton took his family and some of his relations to see it. He was well rewarded when some of the older cowboys recognised the old boss of Outfit 76. They insisted that he drive the Deadwood Coach in which he and his wife used to travel and which was now one of the circus props. This he did and charged through two Indian ambushes with Lord Charles Beresford and Shane Leslie 'riding shotgun'.

When Moreton died at the age of seventy-one, Kipling wrote of him that he had lived 'in every sense except what is called commonsense, very richly and wisely and to his own extreme content, and if he had ever reached the golden crock of his dreams, he would have perished' - a generous and fitting obituary to a remarkable son of Sussex.

Blue Idol Guest House and Quaker Meeting House, Thakeham.
Reproduced by kind permission of Ian H. Abbott.

III   THE COLONISERS AND PLANTERS

If the Elizabethan Age in English history could be described as the Age of Deliverance, the following century certainly deserves the title of the Age of Expansion for it was to see one of the greatest ethnological movements in the history of the English-speaking people. During the course of it, some eighty thousand people, out of a modest population of some three million, left these shores to make a home for themselves on the other side of the Atlantic.

Such a vast movement of population is not precipitated by a solitary influence but is the product of a variety of causes.

Until the victory over the Spanish Armada in 1588, the primary concern of the English had been self-preservation rather than colonial expansion. True, even during those critical years there had been those who dreamed of planting colonies in the New World; men like Richard Grenville; his brother-in-law, Walter Raleigh and the Yorkshireman, Martin Frobisher; but, with the death of Grenville and the eclipse of Raleigh as the Queen's favourite, nothing eventuated. In 1604 King James I concluded a treaty of peace with the Spanish and it was almost as though the flood-gates had been opened. A great surge of colonisation followed and many plantations were made. Virginia was first in 1607 to be followed by Massachusetts - the Pilgrims (as they called themselves) landed on the shores of Massachusetts in 1620, called the spot New Plymouth and founded the city of Boston. New Hampshire and Maine followed in 1622, Maryland in 1634, Rhode Island in 1647, New Jersey, Delaware and North Carolina in 1663. Truly, this half-century in English history was remarkable and laid the foundation of the essentially British character of the North American continent, despite the arrival of thousands of settlers from other European states.

There was another force at work from which came the inspiration to seize the opportunities which the James I peace treaty had opened up - it was that of the pen: the man who wielded it, a parson called Richard Hakluyt.

Towards the end of Elizabeth's reign, he had been appointed chaplain to the English Ambassador in Paris, where he had been forced to listen to the gibes of the French and Portugese representatives at the French Court about England's lack of colonial enterprise. Compared with other seafaring nations the English, so it was claimed, were distinguished only by their 'sluggish security'. For the rest of his life, Hakluyt's aim was to collect and publish accounts of English enterprise; the voyages of the Cabots of Bristol, Drake's circumnavigation of the world, the exploits of Hawkins, Frobisher, Willoughby and others.

In 1582 he published his *Divers Voyages Touching the Discovery of America*. In 1589 came his *Principal Navigation, Voyages and Discoveries of the English Nation*. Through these and subsequent publications, a great impetus was given to the colonisation of the eastern seaboard of North America. But whilst Hakluyt inspired England's seafarers to dream dreams, the City merchants were needed to translate dreams into realities.

Among these 'gentlemen of the counting house' was Thomas Smythe, who became a moving spirit in future ventures. Son of 'Customer' Smythe, an able and shrewd financier, who, towards the end of the previous reign, had farmed the royal customs (with no small benefit both to the Crown and to himself), Thomas formed the Virginia Company by the acquisition of a royal charter. It was divided into two parts: one centred in the City of London and the other in the West Country. Already at the end of 1607, three ships, the *Susan Constant*, the *Godspeed* and the *Discovery*, carrying one hundred settlers and under the command of an adventurer, Captain John Smith, had sailed for Chesapeake Bay. Beside the James River they founded a settlement and called it Jamestown, in honour of the Sovereign. By 1609 a sermon was preached at Whitechapel before the 'adventurers and planters of the Virginia Company'.

Those were the heroic days of colonial enterprise: at the end of the first winter John Smith reported that, out of one hundred who had sailed with him, there remained thirty-eight survivors. Cold, starvation, fevers, untamed forests, wild beasts and wilder men, combined with lack of experience, almost destroyed the first Virginians.

The Virginia Company continued to send supplies and reinforcements but, after six years, Smith reported that, out of the thousand settlers sent out by the Company, eight hundred had died. No wonder Michael Drayton, the poet, was moved to hail the adventurers who were creating transatlantic England with his *Ode to the Virginian Voyage*:

You brave heroic minds, worthy your country's name,
That honour still pursue. Go and subdue,
Whilst loitering hinds lurk here at home with shame.

It is not surprising that many of the first colonists came from Sussex, and to observe that certain characteristics, commonly attributed to Sussex folk, enabled those pioneers to cope with the hardships and the problems which confronted them. One such characteristic has been encapsulated in the Sussex motto 'We won't be druv' which suggests a certain native obstinacy or stubbornness which refuses to surrender easily when people are confronted with problems.

The Sussex character was shaped by the environment in which the people had grown up. In the main they were sons and daughters of farming folk well used to long hours of back-breaking work and the care of livestock. It was these circumstances which helped to shape their character and which enabled them to spread abroad a Sussex 'on which the sun never sets'.

But the county of Sussex was never a rustic island 'entire unto itself', its people shared many typical British characteristics, among which were tolerance, kindliness, suspicion of novelties, distrust of theories unsupported by facts, a tendency to be careless of foreign opinion, a tenacious belief that their own institutions were best for them, and the possession of a buoyant faith in their powers of improvisation or as their critics say, 'muddling through'.

Among these Sussex pioneers was Thomas West, twelfth Baron de la Warr and Lord of the manors of Halnaker and Offington. The latter was in Broadwater, now part of Worthing, at the time a small fishing village in the Broadwater parish.

The West family had become prominent during the reign of Edward III, when, in the year A.D. 1355 under King Edward's son, the Black Prince, they shared in a free-booting expedition against the French. Instead of culminating in the disaster it deserved, it concluded with the famous victory at Poitiers. In the course of that conflict two Sussex soldiers claimed the honour of having captured King John II of France: Henry Pelham and Roger de la Warr, but the honour most probably belonged to Roger, who became third Baron de la Warr.

One of Roger's descendants, the ninth Baron, attended King Henry VIII at that political extravaganza known as 'the Field of Cloth of Gold'. So great was the magnificence displayed by the English and the French nobility, that it was said that they 'carried on their backs their mills, forests and meadows', the implication being that they had mortgaged their estates to appear with their King quite splendidly attired.

Subsequently, de la Warr incurred the royal displeasure by his disapproval of the confiscation of monastic lands and he retired to his manor at Offington. He managed to persuade King Henry's henchman, Thomas Cromwell, 'to spare his poor chantry at Boxgrove' so that he could be buried there. The 'poor chantry' still stands in all its glory at Boxgrove, but Thomas and his wife lie entombed in St. Mary's Parish Church, Broadwater.

One of his descendants, also Thomas, became a director of the Virginia Company and was appointed first Governor of Virginia in 1610, also Captain General of the Crown Colony, and that same year he sailed for Jamestown with reinforcements. Whilst there, he rebuilt the settlement and erected two forts for the protection of the colonists. It was he who arranged for the Indian Princess Pocahontas to visit the Court of King James I in order to be presented to the King by his wife, Lady de la Warr.

On a subsequent voyage to the New World, Thomas died at sea, but his life and work are commemorated in the name given in 1663 to the small new state of Delaware.

* * * * *

It has been suggested that the British 'picked up their empire' in a fit of absentmindedness; this is far from being the truth. Their empire was established through the shedding of much blood, the loss of many lives and much treasure. Their first Crown Colony, Virginia, was no exception to the rule.

One of the problems which the early expeditions encountered was the unsuitability of some of the recruits of the Virginia Company. Of the original party under Captain John Smith, forty-eight were described as gentlemen and only twelve as tillers of the soil. Smith's pragmatic mind quickly recognised that survival depended on the rich Virginian soil and its cultivation. He endowed each settler with three acres of land and commanded that they should 'root, hog or die'. With the ocean behind, and the wilderness in front, self help was plainly the sole means of survival.

* * * * *

Yet another of the states of America was named after a Sussex man, William Penn, who owned an estate at Warminghurst and whose name became famous on both sides of the Atlantic. His father, Admiral Sir William Penn (1621-1670), was a distinguished sailor and described by Samuel Pepys as 'a merry fellow and a pretty good-natured singer of bawdy songs'. Born and reared in Bristol, he trained as a merchant seaman. By the age of twenty-one he had command of a royal ship. At the time of the Commonwealth he was appointed General-at-Sea and was knighted aboard the *Naseby* for his share in the return of Charles II from exile. In 1655 he had captured Jamaica from the Dutch and, before the age of forty, had become the most notable officer in the Navy.

Sir William Penn's son (also named William) was a tall, handsome fellow who enjoyed the friendship of Samuel and Mrs. Pepys. He accompanied them to the playhouse, provoking Samuel to jealousy by the attentions he paid to Mrs. Pepys. Whilst staying on his father's Irish property, William heard a sermon preached by Thomas Loe, an Oxford tradesman. This led him to join the Quakers.

Whilst he was an undergraduate of Christ Church, Oxford, William published a pamphlet with the title *The Sandy Foundations Shaken*. It was nothing less than an attack on the established Church and its doctrines. His punishment was dismissal from Christ Church and imprisonment in the Tower, until his father's influence secured his release. While he was imprisoned he wrote *No Cross, No Crown* which became a Quaker classic.

When Admiral Sir William Penn died in 1670, his son found himself possessed of a fortune. This enabled him to buy an estate at Warminghurst, Sussex, and in 1681 he bought a grant of land in America which eventually took his name and became Pennsylvania.

Following the purchase of his Sussex property in 1671, William Penn married. His bride, Gulielma Maria Posthuma Springett, was the daughter of Sir William Springett of Broyles Court, Ringmer, Sussex.

During the Civil War, Sir William had been associated with Sir William Waller in the capture of Arundel Castle when it was held by the Royalists, and following its surrender to the Parliamentary forces he became Co-Governor of the Castle. Unfortunately he caught typhus and became so ill that his young wife was summoned from London to care for him. Years afterwards, in a letter to her grandson, Springett Penn, she gave a dramatic account of her journey from London to Arundel. She was heavily pregnant at the time she set out and it was winter. They received little help on the way and in several places the coachman found that he had to swim the horses along the flooded roads. At one point the coach overturned on the edge of a precipitous slope. The passengers were fortunate that it slipped no further for, if it had, they would almost certainly have been killed. At long last they reached Arundel only to find it a dismal sight, depopulated, the windows of the houses broken by the siege guns, their lower floors and those of the shops used as stables by Cromwell's horse soldiers.

Lady Springett found her husband delirious, with only his fellow officers as nurses. She tended him for two days and it was only after he died that she was able to weep. After this display of affection which had transcended all considerations of personal safety, Mary Springett was delivered of a child, a girl, who was christened Gulielma Maria Posthuma. It was she, (as mentioned above) who became wife to William Penn. Her mother later married a wealthy Quaker, Isaac Pennington, of Lincoln's Inn Fields.

Whilst living at Warminghurst, William Penn was persecuted on account of his Quaker faith. In 1684 the Chichester Quarter Sessions recorded that William Penn, 'being a factitious and seditious person doth frequently entertain and keep an unlawful assemblage and conventical in his dwelling house at Warminghurst to the terror of the King's liege people'.

Despite these allegations, Penn's friendship with King James II enabled him to get the toleration granted to Roman Catholics extended to include dissenters. Prior to the Toleration Act of 1689, the Sussex Quakers had suffered considerable persecution, many being incarcerated in Horsham

The de la Warr Chantry at Boxgrove.

33

Jail. Some died there and were buried in the Quaker burial ground near Thakeham. In 1691 John Shaw of Shipley Parish offered them the use of a Tudor farmhouse called Slatters. There, William Penn and his fellow Quakers began to meet. His family travelled the four miles to the meeting house in the family coach, drawn (at the speed of two miles an hour) by oxen, the Sussex roads being unfit for coach horses. The new meeting house became known as the Blue Idol, an odd name for a Quaker place of worship. This probably had its origin in the fact that, prior to the Quakers taking possession, the farmhouse had stood empty and was thus 'idle', whilst it was also colour-washed in blue, hence the 'Blue Idol'.

In the year 1682 William Penn had obtained, by letters patent, land in East New Jersey and had founded the Society of Traders of Pennsylvania. The constitution was drawn up at Warminghurst by Algernon Sidney (a grand-nephew of Philip Sidney of Penshurst, Kent), who was to be tried for treason by the notorious Judge Jeffreys and executed on the flimsiest evidence.

The constitution which he drew up afforded freedom of worship to all religions provided that they were monotheist. It also granted the protection of the law to all persons including slaves, though slavery was forbidden.

The aboriginal inhabitants of North America were known as Red Indians, because of the mistaken belief of the original European discoverers that by sailing westwards they had arrived at India. Oppressed by the invaders, the native inhabitants came to hate them. Thus it is not hard to imagine their surprise when they received a letter from one of the white men which addressed them as Friends. The letter apologised for the injustices done to them and promised to pay them for the land which his King had given him. The writer was, of course, William Penn and inaugurated a new era in the relations between white man and red.

Not long afterwards Penn himself arrived and surprised the Indians by his insistence on sitting on the ground with them and sharing a dish of roasted acorns. Still greater was their surprise when the young braves indulged in a display of their physical abilities and the stranger out-leapt them all. Their chief took Penn by the hand and swore on behalf of his people 'to live in friendship with William Penn so long as the sun, moon and stars endure'. For his part, Penn admitted the Indians as citizens of the new-born colony.

Penn had bought into one of the richest mineral regions of North America as well as into a land of vast forests and rich fertile farmland. Already he had financial interests in an iron foundry near Hawkhurst, Kent, and in Pennsylvania he granted letters patent to a fellow Quaker, Thomas Rutter, to build a foundry and furnaces. From these modest beginnings came Pittsburgh, Pennsylvania, to be known as Steel City and the centre of the United States' iron and steel industry.

The house at Warminghurst has been substantially altered but the church, or Steeple House as the Quakers styled it, is still to be seen. It is the only church in Sussex dedicated to the Holy Sepulchre possibly through its proximity to Shipley, owned by the Knights Templar who had a preceptory there. The church was restored in 1959 with beautiful simplicity. The squire's box-pew is still intact whilst the varnish has been stripped from the pews and chancel screen. On the chancel wall is a brass memorial to Sir Edward Shelley, his wife and ten children, with the boys kneeling behind the father and the girls behind Johan, the mother.

*   *   *   *   *

One of the most significant contributions to the embryonic stage of the setting up of the United States of America was made by a man who, until shortly before, had been living in the little county town of East Sussex, Lewes. Tom Paine (1739-1809), Norfolk-born, came to Lewes as an excise officer in 1768, finding lodgings at Bull House with grocer Samuel Olive. After Samuel's death, Tom married Elizabeth, the daughter of the house, in St. Michael's Church in 1771 and took over the running of the business, as grocer and tobacconist.

He played a leading part in the social life of the town on the Bowling Green in the Castle precincts, and as a fearless skater on the wintry dykes - and he was an active participant in Vestry and Town meetings. But his main claim to fame was as a member of the Headstrong Club which met in the *White Hart* to debate burning issues. There he showed a flair for haranguing opponents and developed a questioning attitude to the value of monarchy. He wrote strongly worded pieces on tyranny and injustice, which presaged his commitment to the support of American independence. He published, in 1772, a plea for improved wages for excisemen, *The Case of the Officers of Excise*, which did not endear him to his masters, from whose service he was soon dismissed.

With a failed marriage behind him, Tom Paine sailed for America in 1774, carrying with him a letter of commendation from the great Benjamin Franklin, whom he had met in London. At this time the colonies were feeling the tide of revolt against the pernicious tax on tea. Shortly after his arrival fighting broke out at Lexington. The excellent irregular soldiers gained the advantage, and were soon to seize Bunker's Hill which overlooked Boston. The British regained the initiative, but at so terrible a price in losses, that the commander, Lieutenant-General Thomas Gage, the previously highly respected Governor of Massachusetts was recalled in disgrace. It is a strange coincidence that his family home, Firle Place, was so close to the town of Lewes from which Paine had set out.

Paine was to play an important part in the awakening dream of independence. In 1776, he published *Common Sense*, a history of the events leading to the war, and a clarion call to resistance.

This and the series of pamphlets *Crisis* stiffened the sinews of the colonists; both publications became bestsellers. He held a number of posts in the American government until 1787 when he returned to England. 1791 saw the publication of the first part of his *Rights of Man*, to be followed the next year by the second instalment. This work was prompted as a repudiation of Burke's *Reflections on the Revolution in France*. To escape prosecution he fled to France where he was welcomed warmly and elected a delegate to the assembly known as the Convention. He opposed the execution of Louis XVI which had been advocated by the revolutionary leader, Robespierre. Paine only narrowly escaped the guillotine himself, being reprieved by the overthrow and death of Robespierre.

In 1793 he published *The Age of Reason*, for which he was denounced as an atheist. He returned to America in 1802, but his opposition to Washington and his new views made him almost as unpopular as he had been in England. He had become an extreme radical, although a shrewd political thinker. Much later he was regarded in America, where he died in poverty, as a patriot and as a crusader for democracy. His was an extraordinarily turbulent life for one who had been born a simple country boy, but he certainly made his mark on history. His connection with Lewes is commemorated by an iron plaque on Bull House, in the High Street.

*   *   *   *   *

A curious episode, relating to the colonial expansion of the seventeenth century, concerns a Sussex family called Goffe.

Parson Stephen Goffe, a cleric with Puritan leanings, had been instituted to the livings of Stanmer and Bramber, in the early years of the century. His wife, Deborah (commemorated in Stanmer Church), bore him three sons. The two elder boys graduated from Merton College, Oxford, and were both subsequently awarded the degree of Doctor of Divinity; the second boy, John, became a Fellow of Magdalen College.

The third boy, William, was, in stark contrast to his brothers, 'averse to all kinds of learning'. In consequence he had to enter trade and became apprenticed to a City drysalter - a dealer in drugs, dyes, oils and like products.

During the early summer of 1650, Cromwell occupied Oxford, where the Puritans helped themselves to a variety of university degrees. Cromwell and Fairfax elected to become Doctors of Civil Law but William was content with the degree of Master of Arts (perhaps to avoid the ridicule of his scholarly brothers!). He had scarcely completed his apprenticeship when the Civil War broke out and, apparently having been influenced by his father's Puritan principles, he joined the forces of

Parliament. He also married the daughter of one of Oliver Cromwell's cousins, Frances Whalley (or Walley). Unlike his brother John, who had suffered imprisonment through his refusal to assent to the Solemn League and Covenant, William gained a reputation for his Puritan zeal. He was known as the Prayer-Maker, the Preacher and Presser for Righteousness and Liberty, and soon secured advancement in Parliamentary circles. With the surrender of Charles I he was appointed one of the one hundred and fifty judges for the King's trial and his was the fourteenth signature on the royal death-warrant out of the fifty-nine 'regicides' who signed it.

By 1655 William Goffe had been promoted to the position of one of Cromwell's Major-Generals and made overlord of Sussex, Hampshire and Berkshire, his duty being to fine every Royalist he could discover ten per cent of his income. He was even mentioned as a possible successor to the Protector.

With the Restoration, both Goffe and his father-in-law, Whalley, had to flee the country. They seem to have sought refuge in Lausanne but eventually crossed the Atlantic and landed at Boston, Massachusetts. There they were harried by the authorities (though not very enthusiastically) and had to seek refuge in the outlying settlement of Hadley. Here the wheel of fortune turned in their favour. The little settlement was attacked by Red Indians, and the settlers might all have been massacred but for the military skills of ex-Generals Goffe and Whalley. They managed to organise the colonists' resistance, outflanked the attackers and drove them off. Both the old soldiers lived in Hadley until their deaths and were buried there, side by side.

William's brother, Stephen, became Chaplain to Colonel George Goring's Sussex regiment which fought for the King - an appointment exemplifying the tragic situations created by the Civil War where members of the same family fought on opposite sides. In 1641 Stephen was entrusted with the Thanksgiving sermon to be preached before Colonel Goring's regiment in celebration of the Victory at Nijmegen.

Just as the war divided families so it was with friends. Sir William Campion of Danny, the house near Hurstpierpoint, wrote to his great friend Herbert Morley of Glynde, the principal Sussex leader of the Parliament army: 'I did not rashly or unadvisedly put myself upon this service for it was daily in my prayers for two or three months together to God to direct me in the right way. I believe that you think not that I fight for popery, God knows my heart, I abhor it'.

*　*　*　*　*

Two hundred years after the founding of the Crown Colony of Virginia, another Sussex family became deeply involved in the expansion of the empire. It was at a time when the English-speaking peoples had begun to paint the map of the world red. Some of the hands which wielded the paint-brushes were Sussex born and bred.

One of the most distinguished of these families was that of the Hentys - farmers, brewers and bankers of Worthing. At the junction of Bedford Terrace and Warwick Street (formerly known as Rylands Corner) stood Henty's Bank, partly owned by this Sussex family which was destined to play an important role in the expansion of the British Commonwealth. (After various amalgamations, it finally became absorbed into Lloyds Bank.)

The Henty family consisted of Thomas, his wife and their seven sons and one daughter. The parents farmed the Old Church Farm beside St. Andrew's Church, Tarring, while living at Field Place, and they owned much of the freehold of West Tarring. Thomas was tempted by large grants of land offered by the British Government to those prepared to settle in Western Australia and, as times were bad for agriculture, he decided that a future in the colonies would offer better prospects for his family.

The earliest immigrants to Australia were either members of the civil establishment or of the military forces who had been sent to establish a penal colony in New South Wales. That was in 1788 and these new arrivals were not expected to be more than transients, who would move on to other places, or return to the United Kingdom. Those who remained, unwillingly, in Australia were convicts sentenced to transportation for life.

In the 1820's, the British Colonial Office decided to encourage emigration, and in 1829 and 1836 Western Australia and South Australia were designated as 'free colonies', that is, without penal establishments. To those who emigrated at their own expense, land was made available at little or no cost. The Henty family was among those who would arrive in Western Australia and, as no local labour would be available, they took their own farm workers. A scheme was introduced whereby colonists received a bounty for each person they brought to the colony. Similar arrangements were organised by individuals such as Thomas Peel, others by the South Australian Company.

Thus it was that in 1829 a sailing ship known as the barque *Caroline* (Master - Tewson) sailed from the Sussex Port of Littlehampton. She was a three-masted sailing ship regularly employed in those days on the Australia and New Zealand route. This time she headed for Swan River, Western Australia. Aboard were the Hentys and their three eldest sons, their farm servants (a total of sixty-six souls), their livestock consisting of twelve horses from Lord Egremont's Petworth stud, nine cows and one bull, plus one hundred and eighty-two merino sheep, dressed in flannel coats against the wind, from the stud of George III (fondly known as Farmer George on account of his interest in farming and the improvement of agricultural methods).

The cargo also included a supply of farm implements manufactured by Edward Hollands at his forge in West Tarring High Street. Later on, the same small forge was to supply the Hentys with ploughshares, spades, mattocks, etc. (One of the original ploughshares made by Hollands was sold in 1930 in Australia, for one hundred and ninety pounds.)

In those days such an enterprise was fraught with hardships and perils. The voyage to Australia lasted about seven months during which time food and water had to be provided not only for the passengers but also for the animals.

The new settlers arrived in Western Australia on 12th October 1829. Once ashore, the Hentys faced near catastrophe - a number of their animals became sick, or died, after eating poisonous plants.

The brothers found the country inhospitable, overall, and after two years they sailed east, round South Australia, landing close to an old whaling station, and established themselves at Launceston (Van Diemen's Land, now Tasmania). They sent for the family to join them there. Thomas then chartered the *Forth of Alloway* (Master - Robertson) and with his wife and the rest of the family, namely Charles, Edward, Francis and Jane, together with more sheep, cattle, horses and servants, sailed for Tasmania.

Prevented by government bureaucracy from exchanging the Western Australian grant of land for land in Tasmania, they were forced to rent their Tasmanian farm. Thomas Henty settled on a beautiful property on the banks of the Tamar River and started his sons in their various careers. James became a merchant in Launceston, Charles became manager of the Bank of Australasia and later began a political career. He had married a Sussex girl, Miss Boniface, and whilst in England obtained permission from King William IV to found the Bank of Australasia. Stephen Henty had married a Yorkshire girl from the Vale of Cleveland, one of the richest agricultural districts of England. She was Jane Pace, a native of Stokesley where her portrait is hung in the Town Hall as the first English woman to settle in the state of Victoria.

William Henty, the son who had remained in England and trained as a lawyer, joined the family in Tasmania, later to be elected a member of the Tasmanian Assembly and to become Colonial Secretary from 1857-1865. He returned to England and retired to Brighton where he died in 1881.

Meanwhile, Edward, the most adventurous of the family, investigated the mainland of Australia, across Bass Strait. He anchored off the whaling station at Portland Bay. The land so took his fancy that he decided to stay, but first went back to Tasmania and, in the family schooner *Thistle*, returned to the mainland loaded with stores, livestock, farm implements, seed, fruit trees and vegetables. He landed in 1834, after a terrible voyage of thirty-four days, during which he lost many valuable animals.

The *Thistle* made a second voyage to Portland Bay, bringing fresh supplies and additional colonists. These included Francis, the youngest of the Henty brothers. Edward, at the time, was twenty-four and Francis only eighteen years old. While they waited for their stock to mature, Edward and Stephen engaged in the pursuit of the sperm whale - in those days a hazardous enterprise as it involved hunting the whale from small boats with hand-held harpoons. The mammal was then hauled ashore where it suffocated under its own weight. It was butchered, the blubber being used for its oil, and from the intestines ambergris was extracted for use as a base for perfume. Undoubtedly it was a bloody and dangerous business, calling for strong arms, strong hearts and, no doubt, strong stomachs, but these intrepid sons of Sussex adapted themselves to it and in the first season killed some sixty whales. It is possible that the family schooner, *Thistle*, suitably converted, could have been used for this purpose.

Thus, it came about that by means of a flock of merino sheep which they had brought with them, the Hentys became the pioneers of the pastoral industry of the colony just as, at a later date, they were foremost in commercial enterprise.

The country in which they settled was described by the famous Australian explorer, Major Thomas Mitchell (afterwards Sir Thomas), Surveyor-General of the whole of New South Wales, as 'a place of solemn forests, far stretching pasture, undulating green valleys, gleaming lakes and refreshing water courses' which exceeded his expectations and led him to name it 'Australia Felix'.

It was on 20th October 1835 that Mitchell came across the Henty homestead at Portland Bay and the description he gave of the Wannon Valley, which he and his party had just traversed, decided the Hentys to move a part of their flock there and to build a homestead at Merino Downs. It was Francis Henty who became the owner of the Merino Downs sheep station, some two hundred miles from Melbourne (and who built a house in Melbourne in 1876, naming it Field Place after the name of the house in Worthing where he was born). In order to move the sheep to Merino Downs, the Hentys had to cut their own road through the forest. It was not until 3rd August 1837 that they were able to drive their first flock into the new station. Nine years later they were shipping fat cattle back to Tasmania to supply its population with beef. It was Edward Henty who assembled the plough which was to break Victorian soil.

At the Portland Bay settlement the family had built two large houses, one of which contained twelve rooms. They had invested between eight thousand and ten thousand pounds in the construction of barns, stables, workshops, a dairy and other farm out-buildings, their wool store being the first building erected in Victoria.

Although Edward had encountered considerable difficulties in his initial dealings with the Aborigines, he was able to boast that he had never found it necessary to fire on them.

Among the Sussex families from the neighbourhood of West Tarring who had accompanied the Hentys to Australia were the Chippers, Gees, Rewalls, Bushbys, Sandfords and single men Haybittle, Price, Patterson, Brandon and Gobble.

John and Mary Chipper were two of these new arrivals. Today a bronze plaque identifies the place where John Chipper was involved in an incident on 3rd February 1832 in country near Perth. From local records, it seems that while looking for straying cattle, Chipper and a young boy were attacked by Aborigines. The plaque records that 'John Chipper and Reuben Beacham, a boy of fourteen, while driving a cart from Guildford to York, were attacked by natives. Near this spot, Beacham was killed but Chipper, although speared, escaped and leaped from this rock, now known as Chipper's Leap, and eventually reached Governor Stirling's house at Woodbridge'.

One of the items which John Chipper had brought with him from England was a clock. Made by Edward Nye of Worthing, it now hangs on the wall of the Fremantle Museum.

When the Hentys moved to Tasmania, John Chipper remained at the Swan River settlement where, in due course, he became a bailiff of the Supreme Court - a post he held for twenty-five years. He died in 1871, aged sixty-five.

In 1888 the author of *The First Hundred Years of Australian Settlement* wrote: 'While the present head of the House of Hohenzollern has been building up and uniting the German empire out of old materials, a new empire has been born. There is nothing like it in all the world's history. It has been magical in its celerity. The American colonies crawled into existence as compared with the sudden uprising of these new states'. One of these states came to be named Victoria in honour of the Queen. When the Duke of Gloucester performed the opening ceremony of the Victorian Centenary Celebrations in 1934, it was fitting that he should sail there on H.M.S. *Sussex* as it was a Sussex man, Edward Henty, who had founded the first settlement at Portland Bay a hundred years earlier. Others had come and passed their judgement on the land bordering on Bass Strait. Edward Henty had been the first to visit those shores and to realise their pastoral possibilities. He had no thought of planting a new colony nor of engaging in commercial activities. His aim, and that of his brothers, had been to acquire suitable sheep runs and to cultivate the soil.

The merino sheep originally taken to Australia by the Henty brothers have been bred over the years to a type which is more adaptable to the climatic conditions there. In Goulburn today, an exhibition shows how the breed has been developed since first being introduced into that continent.

The Hentys were certainly unaware that they were laying the foundations of the pastoral industry of sheep farming which, in its turn, led to the building of the great modern city of Melbourne. It was the enterprise, courage and persistence of these sons of Sussex that helped a new civilisation to spring up in the southern hemisphere beneath the Southern Cross.

The life of the Sussex farm labourer, in the early years of the nineteenth century, was often (to quote Thomas Hobbes, writing of an earlier age, in *Leviathan* in 1651) 'poor, nasty, brutish and short'. It was during these same years that there appeared a colonial statesman, Edward Gibbon Wakefield (1792-1862).

Thrown into Newgate for the alleged abduction of his second wife, he wrote *The Letter from Sydney*. In it he exposed the evil effects of transportation on the colonies and sketched out a better system of colonisation. Later, he wrote his *View of the Art of Colonisation*. As a result of his propaganda, many farm labourers who had suffered sadly during the 'hungry forties' decided to try their luck abroad. Among these was a lad from Framfield, near Lewes, called Richard Realf. Instead of heading for Australia he sailed for North America.

This was at the time of the western expansion in North America and the Wild West, which was to become a vital part of the American tradition. Eventually Realf arrived in Kansas.

Those were the days when the Americans were involved in the fight for freedom for every citizen. Their aim was to make the new lands, which were being opened up in the middle and far West, 'free soil'; that is, states where black slavery, long practised in the eastern states, was no longer tolerated.

Young Realf was not Sussex-bred for nought. Behind him lay a long tradition of championship of the weak against the strong, for justice against injustice. As a result, he found himself allied with those famous pioneers of the anti-slavery movement in America: John Brown and his sons.

Born in Connecticut, John Brown had tried to establish in the Virginia mountains a refuge for escaped slaves. The struggle came to a head with the Kansas - Nebraska Bill which proposed to allow local option on the subject of slavery in the new lands and which helped precipitate the Civil War in 1862.

When, after years of terrible slaughter, the northern armies marched to victory over the southern Confederates, they did so singing the song which has immortalised John Brown's name and which was inspired by his martyr's death in 1859.

Like other English villagers, its men-folk were accustomed to long hours of back-breaking toil and their women to the bearing and raising of large families, and to helping their husbands in outdoor tasks. While the men turned their hands to tree-felling, log-cabin-building, hunting and cattle-rearing, the women were well-trained in the arts of butter- and cheese-making and the care of young livestock. Not surprisingly therefore, this Sussex son of toil, Richard Realf, soon settled into the way of life which faced him.

But Realf was confronted, not just with the sort of life to which he had been bred, but with a political situation which demanded he should take sides. He lent his support to the anti-slavery movement. At the same time, the freedom struggle awakened in the young man's breast unsuspected gifts of poetry which he devoted to the cause he had embraced. When he died, sadly by his own hand, he left behind an autobiographical poem which ran:

With sword and song
And speech that rushed up hotly from the heart,
He wrought for liberty ... If missed
World's honours and world's plaudits, still his lips were kissed
Daily by those high angels who assuage
The thirstings of the poets ... for he was born in singing,
And a burden lay mightily on him because
He could not utter to the day what God taught him in the night,
Sometimes, nathless, Power fell upon him and bright tongues of flame
As blessings reached him from poor souls in stress,
And benedictions from black pits of shame.
Nor did he wait till Freedom had become
The popular shibboleth of courtiers' lips.
He smote, when God Himself seemed dumb
And all his arching skies were in eclipse.

The name of Richard Realf was scarcely known in England, nor for that matter in America where his work was mainly done, yet this unknown man from Sussex not only fought against the institution of slavery but 'helped the cause with some noble verses'.

The White Hart in Lewes.

43

F. W. Lanchester (driving) and his brother George in one of their early cars.
Reproduced by kind permission from the Lanchester Collection, Coventry
Polytechnic.

IV   INVENTORS AND INDUSTRIALISTS

Long before it sailed on its Enterprise England, the ultimate fate of the Spanish Armada had been sealed. This was brought about by two Englishmen, Sir John Hawkins and Sir William Wynter.

Hawkins, an experienced ocean-going trader, had been made Treasurer of the Navy Board, the official body which administered the royal ships and dockyards. He had been given this appointment as a result of a paper he had written entitled *Abuses in the Admiralty Touching Her Majesty's Navy*; in it he had exposed corrupt practices which were costing the Crown dear. More than that, he had revolutionary ideas concerning ship design. He strongly believed in the improvement of a warship's sailing qualities through the lengthening of the keel in proportion to the beam, thus enabling a ship to sail closer to the wind. He also wanted to abolish the towering castles in both bow and stern, which were the pride of the early Tudor navy and the Spanish fleet, but which adversely affected the ship's sailing qualities and, in Atlantic gales, could pose a greater threat to the ship's crew than did the enemy. Following these theories he built, and re-built, the Queen's ships and produced a fleet of slim, fast and easy-to-handle ships, more speedy and more weatherly than anything before known.

One of John Hawkins' great rivals was Sir William Wynter, Master of the Queen's Ordnance 1536-1624, yet his ideas on a ship's armament were, in fact, complimentary to his rival's ideas on ship design. He believed in concentrating not so much on 'man-killing' guns but on 'ship-killers' and, through the lengthening of the ship's keel, it became possible to enlarge the ship's broadside (the simultaneous discharge of all the guns on one of its sides).

The part played by the men of Sussex in this naval revolution was to prove critical. The Sussex Weald, along with that of Kent, had become the centre of Europe's gun-making industry. In his *Worthies of Sussex,* old Thomas Fuller had written of how incredible he found it that so many great guns were made in Sussex, an activity which he compared with that of printing, and wondered which of the two had done the most harm. According to the historian, David Hume, in his *History of England*, shipbuilding and the founding of iron cannon were the sole arts in which the English excelled. Sussex-made guns were not only better but also cheaper than continental ones so that laws had to be passed to prevent the export of guns except under licence, and then only through specified ports of which London was the chief. It was claimed that 'the selling of ordnance to strangers (foreigners) to carry overseas has led to the enemy being better furnished with them than our own country's ships are'. Methods of getting round the law were soon forthcoming, one of which consisted in the casting of small-calibre guns (for which export licences could be obtained) but of such diameter that foreign buyers could easily bore them out to take larger shot. The other way to evade the regulations was by smuggling, in which at least one of the leading Sussex families, the Shirleys, was involved (see Chapter I).

One of the reasons why the Weald of Sussex and Kent led the world in the manufacture of iron-cast guns was the presence of vast forests. These provided the charcoal required in those days for smelting the iron ore, which was also found in the Weald and known as 'mine'. The places from which the ore was dug were called mine-pits, and could be up to forty feet in depth.

Two names that arise in connection with the manufacture of the first cast-iron cannon are Ralph Hogge and William Levett. The latter was Rector of Buxted in the sixteenth century but was deprived of his living through his refusal to acknowledge Henry VIII as Head of the Church of England. So he took to the manufacture of ordnance, probably at Oldfield within the Parish of Buxted. In his will Levett bequeathed to his servant the sum of four pounds and 'six tonne of sows' (a sow being a long piece of cast iron made by running the molten metal into a sand-mould). The servant seems to have been Ralph (or Raffe) Hogge (or Huggett), celebrated in the jingle: 'Master Huggett and his man John. They did make the first can-non'. Hogge (or Huggett) mentioned Parson Levett as his predecessor, so it would seem that, having worked for the Rector, he took over the furnace on his master's death. This he worked with Peter Baude, a French expert in the manufacture of bronze guns. In 1573 Ralph Hogge described himself as 'the Quene's Majestyr's gonne-stone maker and gonne-founder of iron'. This means that he manufactured cannon-balls as well as the guns themselves.

In 1574 the house called Marshalls, also the forge and furnace of the same name, near Maresfield, was the property of Ralph Hogge. He must have prospered, for he built himself a house in Buxted with the famous hog-rebus and the date A.D. 1581. A deed of 1588 runs: 'In this house lived Ralph Hog (sic) who, at the then furnace at Buxted, cast the first cannon that was cast in England'. (In the previous year, Hogge had married Margaret Henslow, daughter of the Master of the Game in Ashdown Forest.)

It was not long before the leading families in the county of Sussex became involved in the new industry which produced, not only ordnance, but domestic items such as fire-backs, andirons, anvils, hammers, even grave-slabs, and iron pots and pans, and gressets (vessels used for melting wax for rush-lights). This could have been the bread and butter of the industry for, although armaments yielded big profits, the number of skilled gun-founders was limited. Accordingly, leading families such as the Coverts, the Gratwickes, the Carylls and the Shirleys became not only fellow industrialists but trade rivals, constantly fighting one another in the law courts whilst their employees fought each other on the land. There were times when the area round St. Leonard's Forest must have seemed like an armed camp. (Among these wealthy families who later invested in forge and foundry was William Penn, the famous Quaker.)

In the year of the Armada, Edward Caryll of Shipley and Roger Gratwicke disputed over the digging of ore in St. Leonard's Forest, it being claimed that Gratwicke's servants took only the uppermost veins 'most easy to come by' and thus suffered water 'to drown the said mine'.

Ten years before, Sir William Covert of Slaugham, with Roger Gratwicke, had contended over the let of St. Leonard's Forge and payment for iron sows. In 1587 Gratwicke was again at war with Covert and Carryll, it being alleged they had conspired not only to deprive him of some of his ironworks but also 'by force and might, all my wealth and substance', his stock of iron and ore being assessed at four thousand pounds. Carryll's servants had been 'armed and apparelled in war-like manner with swords, daggers and staves with which they did wound and beat Gratwicke's servants as they worked at the ironworks and had violently taken great quantities of ore and carried it to the works of Carryll'.

On another occasion the rearmost ox-wain, carrying ore to Gratwicke's furnace, was attacked. Gratwicke's drovers ran to the rescue, armed with ox goads, and in the *melee*, Henry Wood was so wounded that they had to cut off his shirt tails for bandages to prevent his bleeding to death. The attackers also took his sword, worth at least twenty shillings.

This enmity was not confined to the furnace areas, for a Caryll servant, Thomas Marsh, was accused of assaulting Richard Whitebread whilst the latter was bound for church in Horsham. (Evidently there was nothing sacred in those bitter conflicts.) With dagger drawn he chased him into the house of Thomas Champion.

Both Roger Gratwicke and his son (also Roger) became wealthy men, as did the Carrylls and Coverts, with the result that each of these families was taxed one hundred pounds for the defence of Sussex when the Armada threatened and the Duke of Parma awaited a chance to cross the Channel with his invading army.

Roger II built the furnace at Gosden near Cowfold, claiming ore from the mine-pits, only to have his sole right to mine challenged by Walter Covert and Edward Caryll. They alleged that his mine-pits were wastefully operated and produced more ore than he could use, and that they only took what he could not use and what his men left behind. All this feuding was in progress while Sussex and England stood in dire peril from the invader. At the same time Sussex was able to muster four thousand foot and two hundred and fifty horse for the defence of their religion and land.

Another ironmaster of the sixteenth century was Richard Woodman of Warbleton who employed a hundred workmen. Unfortunately, he professed the Protestant faith, strong in the reign of Edward VI, and refused to recant when (on the death of her brother) Mary Tudor assumed the throne.

Woodman even dared to admonish the local rector for his 'Romish practices'. The result of all this was that he was arrested by the sheriff's men and locked in the church tower. He escaped but was eventually recaptured and, in Lewes High Street along with nine others, was burned to death. Out of the two hundred and eighty Protestant martyrs during the reign of 'Bloody Mary', no less than thirty-three were Sussex men and women. One of the fire-backs still in existence shows a man and a woman tied back-to-back to the stake while the flames raged around them - a grotesque form of ornament, surely?

All this industrial activity was not universally popular. Even in those far off days there were some who regretted the threat to the environment. Michael Drayton (1563-1631), the poet, was such a one. In his *Poly-Olbion*, a great topographical poem, he pleaded for the conservation of the Wealden forests:

Jove's oak, the war-like ash, veined elm, the softer beech,
Short hazel, maple plain, light asp and bending wych,
Tough holly and smooth birch, must altogether burn.
What should the builder serve, supplies the forger's turn,
When under public good, base private gain takes hold,
And we, poor woeful woods, to ruin lastly sold.

Others complained that the timber required to build houses, ships, barrels, roof tiles and other domestic requirements, was in short supply because of the vast quantities consumed by the iron foundries, whilst it took fifty Sussex oak trees to build one three-decker ship!.

Others attacked the 'gonne-makers' for what they regarded as an assault on ancient notions of chivalry. Thomas Fuller, in his *Worthies*, saw the gun as an instrument of cruelty which 'subjected valour to chance'. Nor did the gun give quarter, which the sword often did. At the same time he admitted that, since the advent of the gun, victories had been won with fewer casualties.

Nevertheless, the devastation of the woodlands continued until, in the year 1760, Abraham Darby discovered how to replace charcoal with coke in his blast furnaces. By that time, the forests of the Weald had been denuded, their roads ruined by the transport of ore and pig iron and the pastoral scenery of the present day almost destroyed and replaced by a man-made 'black country'.

*   *   *   *   *

To confine Sussex industry to the almost forgotten iron and glass manufactures would be unrealistic. From the earliest times the county's chief industry has been that of farming. Sussex cattle and Sussex sheep have achieved an international reputation and no Sussex man has done more to make this possible than John Ellman (1753-1812) of Glynde.

He organised his establishment on patriarchal lines, all his unmarried servants being lodged and boarded under his own roof. If, and when, they married, each one was set up with enough grassland on which to keep a cow and a pig, plus sufficient land on which to maintain an allotment for the production of various crops - potatoes, vegetables and the like.

It was John Ellman, the improver of the Southdown breed of sheep, who was responsible for its reputation as the best of breeds as regards both wool and meat. Indeed, he came to be so highly regarded as an authority on agricultural and farming matters that the Duke of Bedford preferred to talk farming with John Ellman rather than attend the Prince Regent's revels in Brighton.

Not only did Sussex become famous for an improved breed of sheep, it also became the home of the Arab horse, the introduction of which was due to the work of Wilfrid Scawen Blunt and his wife. Together they had travelled in Arabia, buying Arab mares and stallions whose pedigrees went back down the centuries. These beautiful animals formed the beginnings of the famous Crabbet stud, now dispersed, although part of it was owned by Blunt's grand-daughter, Lady Anne Lytton, of Newbuildings Place, Horsham. She was elected President of the Arab Horse Society and in this capacity, towards the end of her days, toured the United States of America.

* * * * *

Just as Ralph Hogge and his French colleague, Peter Baude, discovered how to cast cannon in Sussex iron, so it was to Sussex that England had to look for the inventor of the first English motor car, thus enabling (to use Kipling's words) the dawn of a new age:

When men grew shy of hunting stag,
For fear the Law might try 'em,
The Car put up an average bag
Of twenty dead *per diem*,
Then every road was made a rink
For Coroners to sit on,
And so began, in skid and stink,
The real blood-sport of Britain!

The inventor in question was F. W. Lanchester whose creation came to bear his name.

Frederick, or F. W. (as he was known), was the son of Henry Lanchester, the architect of a considerable portion of Hove - the developing suburb of Brighton. It was he who designed Grand Avenue, and the First, Second, Third and Fourth Avenues which flank it.

Of his two sons, Henry followed in his father's steps and became the designer (along with E. A. Rickards) of the famous Central Hall, Westminster, as well as the new buildings of Leeds University, Cardiff Town Hall and Law Courts. Frederick attended what was then known as the Hartley Institute (later the University), Southampton, from where he proceeded to the Royal College of Science, London. There, one of his fellow students was H. G. Wells, but Frederick never cared much for him.

F. W. left college without taking his degree and set up as a mechanical engineer near Birmingham in partnership with a brother called George. In 1896 he produced his first experimental car: a two-cylinder air-cooled model with a 5 h.p. engine.

Five years later came what was, at the time, a technical masterpiece - his 10 h.p. Lanchester - and by 1905 no fewer than four hundred were on the British roads. It was years ahead in design with a uniquely vibration-free engine which drove the rear wheels through a propeller shaft and a worm gear on the rear axle. Its suspension consisted in cantilever springs all round. The original steering was by a tiller, later to be replaced by the wheel. Every part of this car (except for the rubber tyres) was designed and manufactured by Lanchester.

F. W. and Rudyard Kipling were friends, drawn to each other by two mutual interests: poetry and motor cars. What Rudyard thought of his friend's poems is not known but he would certainly have approved some of the sentiments they expressed. For instance, in 1937 one poem appeared in the journal *Engineering*. It was at a time when there was much agitation for disarmament. F. W. attacked its advocates and urged negotiation from strength. He wrote:

Thou knowest there is no easy way to peace;
No road save that the brave and strong may win and hold;
So, in the sacred cause of peace, must we be strong,
Fearless, with faith in Thee and our high destiny.

Nor was Lanchester without a sense of humour, so that when a Professor F. Soddy sent him a poem entitled *The Kiss Precise*, his response was:

The Kiss Precise, the maiden said
Is not a lover's portion
For clearly, at the contact point,
There must be no distortion,
But when true lovers kiss, we know
Body presses on body,
So take away your chilly kiss,
Professor Soddy!

As well as his poetry, F. W. Lanchester directed his interests to aerodynamics, a subject about which he had dreamed from his college days. When, in 1906, *The London Times* was alleging that all attempts at 'artificial aviation' (presumably by heavier-than-air machines) were not only dangerous to human life but foredoomed to failure, Lanchester was writing his *Aerial Flight* which was to prove a foundation for future scientists with wind-tunnels at their disposal. Like R. J. Mitchell, the designer of the famous Spitfire in a later generation, Lanchester developed his *Vortex Theory of Flight* by the observation of seagulls.

Rudyard Kipling bought one of the early Lanchester 10 h.p. cars and one day, as he never drove himself, made arrangements for the inventor to drive him from Rottingdean over to Worthing to visit his old friend, the literary critic, W. E. Henley, who was living in St. George's Lodge. As Amelia (the name Rudyard had given his new car) cruised along Chesswood Road she ground to a halt; F. W. had to spend two hours dismantling and re-assembling his creation until, in the end, according to Kipling, 'she spat boiling water over our laps, but we stuffed a rug into the geyser and so spouted home'.

This incident did not sever the bonds of friendship between the poet and the inventor and, years afterwards, Lanchester was sending his cars down to Burwash for Kipling to experiment with. One model, a two-cylinder job of 18 h.p., was christened by Kipling 'Jane Cakebread', a notorious Cockney character who had ninety-three convictions in a single year for being drunk and disorderly. That very car was the subject of a pointed telegram which Kipling sent to Lanchester's Birmingham works. It read: 'Jane disembowelled on village green Ditchling. Pray remove your disorderly experiment'. A later Lanchester, Amelia, let her master down on a visit to Henry James, after he had boasted of the superiority of a form of transport of which James was highly suspicious. Kipling recorded that she was 'took with a cataleptic trance...and abode in Rye stark and motionless'. He regarded Amelia as a bitch and said of her that she was the 'petrol-piddling descendant of untold she-dogs'. Kipling nicknamed all his cars. Having later converted to Rolls each became The Duchess.

In 1909, Lanchester was appointed Consulting Engineer and Technical Advisor to the English Daimler Company and, in this capacity, enabled them to solve development problems associated with their famous Knight Double-Sleeve Valve engine.

F. W. and his brother George lived their later years in St. Bernard's Road, Olton, Birmingham, where their bachelor existence was made comfortable by the presence of the lady who had once been their nurse. F. W. died in 1946 in relative poverty, but surely this young man from Sussex has the right to be hailed as one of the pioneers, not only in the realm of aerial flight, but in the development of the British car industry.

*   *   *   *   *

Magnus Volk was the Brighton born son of an immigrant German clockmaker. He became an archetypal inventor, turning his ingenuity in many directions, from telephones and electric lighting to fire-alarms and electric launches. His experimentation cost him dear, and at one stage he was declared bankrupt. In 1883 he inaugurated a sea-front railway from the Aquarium to the Chain Pier, and the following year it was extended to Paston Place. It still features as a tourist attraction along Madeira Drive as far as Black Rock.

But what must have been one of the most bizarre forms of transport ever devised ran between Paston Place, Brighton, and the gap at Rottingdean, with, later, an intermediate stop at Ovingdean Gap. It was known officially as 'The Brighton and Rottingdean Seashore Electric Railway'.

The 'Daddy Long-Legs' railway as it was nicknamed was a more adventurous concept than his sea-front line, running as it did on tracks laid on the foreshore and hoisted to above high water level by stilt-like legs. The twin tracks were fixed to concrete blocks fixed to the chalk abrasion platform, the overall gauge being 18' The carriage, held 24' above the bogeys was called 'The Pioneer', and the enclosed saloon had decking around it with more promenade space on top. It was powered by electricity carried through an overhead wire. The Board of Trade insisted that it carry a lifeboat and lifebelts, that its maximum load was 150 passengers and that it travelled at no more than 8 m.p.h. Nor was it allowed to operate in rough weather.

At low tide the whole mechanism could be seen, but at high tide the saloon was carried on its stilts not far above water level. Operations were beset with problems, for only a week after the inaugural run on 28th November 1896, a tremendous storm, which destroyed the chain pier in Brighton, also caused the Banjo Groyne terminal jetty of the railway to collapse. 'Pioneer' broke loose from its moorings at Rottingdean and was wrecked, but the terminal there survived. Rebuilding of the carriage and of the Banjo Groyne terminal allowed the railway to re-open the following July. Edward, Prince of Wales, made two return trips in one day in February 1900 and later the same year a 'request stop' was constructed at Ovingdean gap.

The Rottingdean jetty was constructed of steel girders which projected 100 yards out from the cliff. The pier head stood 30´ clear of high water and there were steps down to the landing stage. Beneath the pier was the 60 kilowatt, 500 volt steam generator. A funnel carried away the fumes and smoke, but this pollution elicited vigorous complaint from one of the newly elected parish councillors, Lady Georgiana Burne-Jones. It seemed not to worry her nephew, Rudyard Kipling, who, with his children, enjoyed fishing from the pier head.

After a number of restrictions imposed by Brighton Council, which wanted Magnus Volk to divert the line for Groyne extensions, the line became less viable and was eventually closed in 1901. 'Pioneer' was moored at the Ovingdean stage until 1910 when it was scrapped. Rottingdean Pier was demolished at the same time. At low tide many of the concrete blocks, which anchored the track are still visible. Magnus Volk's grave may be seen in Ovingdean Churchyard, fittingly just inland halfway along the route of his flamboyant invention.

Angela Thirkell recalls the arrival of 'Pioneer' in her delightful memoir of childhood days, *'Three Houses'*:

'By this time a little crowd was collecting on the pier and if my brother and I could find a suitable escort (for we were never allowed to do anything on our own, possibly with reason), we had permission to join it. An Uncle, or good-natured Julian Ridsdale, would volunteer to look after us and off we would go to see the arrival of the Daddy Long-Legs. This was the most preposterous machine which came on railway lines through the sea from Brighton every day. Huge blocks of concrete had been laid in the sea with lines on them and along these rolled a kind of elevated platform with four immensely long legs ending in great boxes with wheels inside them. It was more like a vision of the Martians than anything you ought to see at a peaceful seaside village. We were never allowed to go in it, partly because no grown-up thought it amusing enough to go with us and partly because it had a habit of sticking somewhere opposite the ventilating shaft of the Brighton main sewer and not being moved till nightfall. When it had discharged its passengers at the pier it took on a fresh load and stalked back again to Brighton leaving us in gaping admiration'.

The 'Daddy-Long-Legs' Railway.

Pioneer at Rottingdean pier.

Rottingdean v. Sussex County side at Rottingdean in 1986.
Reproduced by kind permission of Rottingdean Cricket Club.

V   THE CRICKETERS

The county of Sussex has long been a cradle for 'the meadow game with the beautiful name' - cricket.

Many of the village greens, which nurtured the game's development, were in Sussex and in the neighbouring counties of Kent, Surrey and Hampshire. It was there that a race of Englishmen was developed who became not only distinguished exponents of the game, either with bat or ball or both, but also some of the most colourful and staunch members of 'the bulldog breed'. Frederick William Lillywhite, born in the tiny village of Westerton near West Hampnett, West Sussex, was one of this breed.

His epitaph in Highgate Cemetery extols him as 'one who taught, both by precept and example, a sport in which the blessings of youthful strength and spirits may be innocently enjoyed, in the exercise of the mind, the discipline of the temper and the general improvement of the man'.

Lillywhite is remembered as, if not the originator of the art of round-arm bowling, then certainly the perfecter of it. At the time it met with many objections, especially from the Australians who were among its early victims, but by 1828 it had been accepted.

During his twenty-seven years of active cricket, it was claimed that Lillywhite bowled no fewer than twelve 'wides' and took a myriad wickets at the cost of seven runs apiece. When his fame as a bowler was established, he was ready to bowl at any gentleman, whether young or old, who was prepared to pay him five shillings for the privilege.

The Cricketers Arms in Duncton has long been famous because John Wisden, author of the *Cricketers' Almanack* (still the cricketer's Bible), was once its landlord. His nephew, James Wisden, played in the first Test Match against Australia and in several others. But Duncton's most famous son was Jem Broadbridge. It was probably he who introduced overarm bowling in 1815, and although the style was prohibited by the Revised Laws the following year, it was gradually accepted as the norm. He and Lillywhite were the first great partnership for Sussex. When batting, it became Broadbridge's custom to celebrate each big hit by calling for a mug of ale. A player who intimidated batsmen long before 'bodyline' bowling ever came into prominence was Jutton. In the 1790's, in the days of underarm bowling, he took a delight in aiming at the batsman's unprotected shins. It seems that unsporting tactics are nothing new!

Another famous fast bowler of former days was George Brown, born in Sompting, near Worthing. He was a tailor by trade, stood six feet three inches and had fathered nineteen children. When he bowled for Brighton, the long-stop, one Dench, used to protect himself with a straw-padded chest protector. It was whilst Brown was bowling at Lord's (or so they say) that a spectator tried to stop one of his deliveries by dropping a coat on it. The ball went right through the coat and killed a dog! Cricket enthusiasts, it seems, can match fishermen in their ability to tell tall tales. As well as being a fine bowler, George Brown, when batting, thought in sixes, so that it was written of him:

A fine slashing hitter, he counts it a crime
To get any less than six runs at a time.

In complete contrast to long-stop Dench stands wicket-keeper Thomas Box, from Ardingly who, even when facing the fastest bowlers, disdained the protection of gloves - one of the advantages no doubt of being one of the 'horny-handed sons of toil'.

* * * * *

What must surely be the earliest reference to cricket in Sussex is to be found in the Easter Presentements 1662 by the Churchwardens of Boxgrove. They accused Anthony Ward, the servant of the Vicar, and Edward Hartley, of playing cricket during Evensong on Sunday 28th April. Worse was to come, for on the following Sunday the Vicar had to present Hartley and four other men, aided and abetted by both Churchwardens, in spite of warnings, of playing cricket in the churchyard. He accused them thus; 'First it is contrary to the Seventh Article; secondly for that they use to break windowes with the ball; and thirdly, that for a little child had like to have her braynes beaten out with a cricket bat'. An amazing indictment, although it must be remembered that there were unlikely, then, to be gravestones to impede the progress of the game. Why did the Churchwardens suddenly rebel? How did a small girl wander on to the pitch closely enough to come into contact with the bat? Sadly we shall never know.

* * * * *

Sussex cricket has long been indebted not only to its players but also to its patrons. Among these early supporters was the Prince Regent, later King George IV. He has been greatly vilified by historians, by his own family, and by his contemporaries, yet at least some of the popularity which the game achieved was due to his interest and patronage. Not only did he occasionally join in the game 'with great affability and condescension', but, by giving it the stamp of royal approval, he enabled cricket to take its place as a truly national pastime. It is surely worth noting that this took place at a time when cruel sports, such as bull- and bear-baiting and the hunting of tame deer released from captivity, were the order of the day, not to mention dog- and cock-fighting.

In 1783 the Prince Regent had a ground laid out in Brighton, partly on what is called The Level and partly on Park Crescent. In 1823 it became Ireland's Gardens and many famous names performed there before it removed, in 1848, to the Brunswick ground in Hove; so close to the sea that many a great hit landed therein. The present county ground was opened in 1872.

Earlier patrons of Sussex cricket included Sir William Gage of Firle Place, from a family famous for the introduction of the greengage plum to England. Another aristocratic patron was the second Duke of Richmond, whose team represented Slindon village and included the famous Newland brothers, Adam and Richard; the latter to become known as the father of English cricket. The third Duke captained Sussex in 1768 when they lost to the Hambledon Club from the neighbouring county of Hampshire. He atoned for this lapse by introducing horse-racing to the beautiful Goodwood Course.

*   *   *   *   *

In those earlier days, cricket matches were played for substantial stakes and it seems that a game without a wager was like an egg without salt. Thus, we can read of how the gentlemen of the Weald played the gentlemen of the South Coast for a hundred guineas and won by 7 runs. This was small beer compared with the stakes involved in the match between Sussex and an Epsom club, which included a famous batsman of the time, Lord Francis Beauclerk, and which was played for a thousand guineas. In that notorious age of gambling for high stakes, gentlemen wagered gold rings, gold chains and watches on the outcome of a single game.

In 1764, on Henfield Common, an East Sussex team took on the Arundel side 'for a considerable sum'. With so much money at stake it is not surprising to find that team discipline was strict. In 1837 the rules of Henfield Club required that in all practice matches, 'every member not fetching 5 runs in each innings should forfeit one penny and the same for missing a fair catch'. (It is not hard to imagine the arguments which would ensue as to what constituted 'a fair catch'.) Another rule warned that 'any player degrading himself by getting liquor before the match is played, is under forfeit of two shillings and sixpence'. In 1830, the agricultural workers of Sussex petitioned for two shillings and threepence a day in winter and two shillings and sixpence in summer, for married men, and one shilling and ninepence and two shillings for bachelors. Thus, in those days, if you played cricket, a set of 'butterfingers' constituted an expensive handicap.

Rottingdean has an exceptionally long history as the home of a cricket club. The earliest match of which there is a record was played on Wednesday 28th June 1758, although the game was almost certainly played there before this. The ground was then in Balsdean Bottom, some way inland below Height barn. The game was advertised as a 'great match at CRICKET for a guinea a man'. The teams widely drawn for it were between Newick, Chailey, Lindfield and Hamsey against Lewes, Brighthelmstone and Rottingdean. Then, as for generations to come, the local team was led by a member of the Beard family - the village squires.

Sometime later the pitch was moved to stand alongside the windmill on the cliff-top at Beacon Hill. As there were no boundaries and the field sloped steeply on either hand, it was not the most suitable site for the game. There is a note of one occasion when a hit sent the ball downhill eastward to Hog Plat. A relay of fielders returned the ball to the wicket keeper who hurled it at the stumps, missed, and watched the errant ball start off down the other side of the hill. The batsmen, who kept on running, must have covered three-quarters of a mile before the ball was dead and the 67 runs 'in the bag' (or notched up on the stick, which was how they used to score). Another hazard of the game on the cliff was the fact that occasionally play had to be held up because a ship appeared behind the bowler's arm.

In those days refreshment was a vital element in the entertainment. 'Civil John' Sladescane, Landlord of The Plough supplied the food and gallons of beer, shandygaff and ginger beer - all set out in a canvas booth near the mill. If the ball hit the tent it was regarded as a boundary or, in local terms, a 'boother'. Cricket continued on Beacon Hill until the outbreak of the Great War. The present ground is secure in a fold of the Downs - a very distinctive and delightful setting - alongside the road to Falmer.

Alfred Mynn, the cricketer, representing June in an almanac of twelve sports.

Cricket.

Thank God who made the British Isles
 And taught me how to play,
I do not worship crocodiles
 Or bow the knee to clay!

Give me a willow wand and I,
 With hide and cork and twine,
From century to century
 Will gambol round my Shrine.

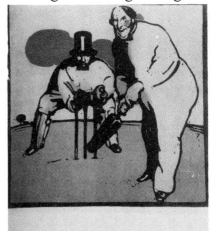

June.

It is particularly appropriate that Rudyard Kipling should have written a verse about cricket in Rottingdean where the cricketing tradition was so strong. He collaborated with William Nicholson in 1897 in a publication called *An Almanac of Twelve Sports* in which each month was represented by a woodcut and a verse. That for June featured Alfred Mynn at the wicket. He was a famous Kent all-rounder of the 1830's and 1840's who weighed some 18 stone.

*　*　*　*　*

Another stronghold of Sussex cricket was the village of Slindon, made famous by the Newland brothers. Their ancestral home, Newlands, still stands beyond the village pond. Here Richard Newland, the father of cricket, taught his nephew, Richard Nyren, the art of the game. In turn Nyren made the men of Hambledon one of the most famous teams in the country. He was described as one of the finest bats of his time and, in 1745, made 88 runs for England against Kent.

Just off the Cowfold - Bolney road lies the hamlet of Oakendene, the birthplace of several cricket giants, among them Boorer and Vallance. In 1792 they helped Brighton beat the newly-founded Marylebone Club by making 66 and 68 not out, respectively, in the second innings.

William Wood, from the same village, was acclaimed in his day as the best bowler in England. He perfected his skill by always having a ball in his pocket as he walked about his farm. Sighting a suitable target, he would bowl at it, and he trained his dog to 'field' the ball.

Nor was cricket the preserve of men. Bury village boasted a women's team which, after the married women had beaten the single women by 88 runs, challenged any female team in the county to a match.

Another distinguished lady player was Miss Lucy Ridsdale of the Dene, Rottingdean, who married Stanley Baldwin and thus became wife to England's Prime Minister.

*　*　*　*　*

Sussex cricket has long abounded in legends and legendary figures, possibly because the game reached its high noon at the same time as the British people were, almost unconsciously, building the greatest empire known to history. Games were marked by keen rivalry as village took on village with fierce partisanship. They were usually completed by a visit to the local hostelry where, over much-needed refreshment, the match was relayed whilst recollections of former nonpareils were evoked (and embroidered). In those halcyon days people were not afraid of heroes and hero-worship and the game produced many idols with every county having its roll of heroes of the bat and ball, the willow and leather.

Sussex has made an outstanding contribution to national heroes of the game. C. B. Fry came from an old Mayfield family, and was such a god-like figure that H. S. Altham wrote of him 'He could, alike in form and feature, have stepped out of the frieze of the Parthenon'. He took a First in Classics at the end of his third year at Oxford but, amazingly, achieved only a Fourth in his final year. As though to make amends, for the rest of his life he excelled at everything. Not only a man of letters, C. B. was the epitome of the all-rounder in sport - world record holder of the long-jump, player of international soccer for England and, above all, a flawless cricketer from whose bat flowed century after century. He was idolised by a generation of youth. He declined the offer of the monarchy of Albania, taking instead command of the Training Ship 'Mercury' on the Hamble. His contemporary was the Indian princeling K. S. Ranjitsinhji whose scoring ability was equally stylish. These heralded a succession of names which became legendary: A. E. R. Gilligan, Duleepsinhji, and that special Sussex breed, the cricketing family, such as the Tates, the Langridges, the Parks and the Wells.

Much earlier, a poetic appreciation was penned by Reynell Cotton, a schoolmaster cleric and Rudgwick man:

Ye strikers observe when the foe shall draw nigh
Mark the bowler advancing, with vigilant eye;
Your skill all depends on distance and sight:
Stand firm to your scratch; let your bat be upright.

Ye fieldsmen look sharp lest your pains ye beguile,
Move close like an army, in rank and in file.
When the ball is returned, back it sure, for I trow
Whole states have been ruined by one over-throw.

Ye bowlers take heed; to my precepts attend,
On you the whole fate of the game must attend,
Spare your vigour at first, nor exert all your strength,
But measure each step and be sure pitch a length.

*Rottingdean Mill on Beacon Hill,
close by the old village cricket pitch.*

Educated at Winchester in 1730, Cotton took Holy Orders and became master of Hyde Abbey School in that city. He died in 1779 but not before he had given his verdict on the game he so appreciated and loved:

Since Ajax fought Hector in sight of all Troy
No contest was seen with such fear and such joy.

*   *   *   *   *

Described by J. M. Barrie as the best story about cricket or any other game, is Hugh de Selincourt's *The Cricket Match*. The author was a critical journalist who lived near Pulborough and at one time captained Storrington's village team.

In 1924 he conceived the idea of using the structure of a village cricket match as the basis for a novel. He was convinced that cricket was the greatest game and village cricket its supreme expression. The match is played at Tillingfold, the name de Selincourt gave to Storrington, and has been described as a 'comic melodrama played out between breakfast and supper'. First published by Jonathan Cape in 1924, it was republished by Oxford University Press in 1979 and has achieved the status of a minor classic. It has also been adapted into a delightful play for television.

Another classic account of the delights of a village cricket match is to be found in A. G. Macdonell's *England their England*. The team immortalised is 'The Invalids', a motley collection of men of letters brought together by Sir Jack Squire, a poet, and founder and editor of the London *Mercury*. In 1920 they were the guests, at Rodmell, near Lewes, of Jim Allison, a wealthy Australian publisher whose hospitality was legendary. The visiting team had no interest in the rural preoccupations of the village side but the cricketers played their match in a spirit of jovial rivalry under a warm summer sun. The narrow street overflowed with the cars of the supporters, among whom was Hilaire Belloc ponderously attired in an unseasonal black cape. Defeat for 'The Invalids' was attributed to over-indulgence at lunch and the volume of beer provided by their generous host. There is a clear parallel between the fictional match set in a Kentish village and the real one in the Ouse valley.

St. George's Lodge, Worthing.

'Sir, we are a nest of singing birds', so wrote Dr. Samuel Johnson of those sons of Pembroke College, Oxford, who were poets. The same could be said of the county of Sussex which, for centuries, has either produced or sheltered a host of poets, some of whom have achieved lasting fame. One of the most compelling Sussex poets was Rudyard Kipling, who in *Sussex* wrote;

God gave all men all earth to love,
But since our hearts are small,
Ordained for each one spot should prove
Beloved over all;

and then in the next stanza concluded:

Each to his choice, and I rejoice
The lot has fallen to me
In a fair ground - in a fair ground -
Yea, Sussex by the sea!

- a celebration shared by many others. But Rudyard Kipling was more than a poet, because his versatility amounted to genius. In addition to being a best-selling poet, he was also an author of children's books, a novelist, and a supreme master of the short story. He enriched the English language with more memorable quotations than any other writer of his time.

   Rudyard Kipling was born in Bombay on December 30th 1865, son of John Lockwood Kipling, an artist and teacher of Architectural Sculpture, and his wife Alice. She was one of the Macdonald sisters, talented beauties, of whom four married remarkable men: Sir Edward Burne Jones, Sir Edward Poynter, Alfred Baldwin and John Lockwood Kipling himself. Young Ruddy's earliest years were blissfully happy in an India full of exotic sights, sounds and smells, but at the tender age of 5 he was brought back to England to stay with a foster family in Southsea, where he was desperately unhappy. The experience would colour some of his later writing.

   During those years, and subsequently when attending United Services College at Westward Ho! near Bideford, he would stay during the holidays with his Aunt and Uncle, Georgiana and Edward Burne-Jones at their home, The Grange, North End Road in Fulham. Later, in *Something of Myself*, he fondly recalled his time spent there: '..and arriving at the house would reach up to the open-work   65 iron bell-pull on the wonderful gate that let me in to all felicity. When I had a house of my own and The Grange was emptied of meaning, I begged for and was given that bell-pull for my entrance, in the hope that other children might also feel happy when they rang it'. It still hangs in the porch at Bateman's, a now mute witness to his genuine concern for the young.

Rudyard also stayed for a few days with the Burne-Jones at their holiday home in the seaside village of Rottingdean, near Brighton before returning to India to take up a career with the *Civil and Military Gazette* in Lahore. In his limited spare time he wrote many remarkable poems and short stories which were printed alongside his reports. When these were collected and published as books, they formed the basis of his early fame. On his return to England he was lionised in literary society. He later married Caroline Balestier, sister of an American friend and collaborator; he and Carrie set up home in Brattleboro, Vermont, where their children Josephine and Elsie were born.

Following a bitter quarrel with his brother-in-law, Beatty, Rudyard and his family left for England. In Queen Victoria's Diamond Jubilee year of 1897 they settled in Rottingdean, which was to be their home for the next five years and where their son John was born. A happy family life allowed Kipling to complete some of his most memorable works - *Kim, Stalky & Co.* and *Just So Stories* together with poems including *Recessional, The Way through the Woods* and *The Absent-minded Beggar*.

The joy and fulfillment were not to last for, after the tragic death of their elder daughter, Josephine, during a return visit to the United States, The Elms at Rottingdean was so full of bitter-sweet memories that Rudyard could no longer bear its associations. As he was also the target of much tourist curiosity the Kiplings resolved to find a new home offering seclusion. Their search ended at Bateman's. The lovely house in the valley of the little River Dudwell, below the ridge on which Burwash stands, gave them peace and the love of a landscape which contrasted markedly with the Downland he so much admired. No writer has ever written more magically about the Sussex countryside either in poetry or prose. His poem, *A Three Part Song*, expresses his delight:

I'm just in love with all these three,
The Weald and the Marsh and the Down countree.
Nor I don't know which I love the most
The Weald or the Marsh or the white Chalk Coast!

and it goes on to extol the virtue of each in three more simple stanzas.

The Kiplings travelled widely, Rudyard being a dedicated motorist, but after the loss of their son, John, a subaltern killed at the Battle of Loos in 1915, they relied more and more on the peace offered by their wooded valley. Kipling died a few days before his friend, King George V, in January 1936.

The Elms, Rottingdean.

Batemans, Burwash.

Bateman's, given to the National Trust on Carrie's death three years later, still radiates the love they felt for the mellow sandstone house, with its glorious garden and mill set 'as snugly as a cup in a saucer' in the valley under Pook's Hill.

Burne-Jones was a friend of Dante Gabriel Rossetti but never became one of the pre-Raphaelite Brotherhood which Rossetti is reputed, by some, to have founded.

Rossetti came to Sussex at the instigation of Barbara Leigh-Smith (a cousin of Florence Nightingale) following the example of her father, Benjamin Leigh-Smith M. P., who was a patron of the arts. She was also a pioneer feminist believing that a brighter future for women depended on better education being made available to them.

With this in mind she founded a grammar school for girls near her London home in Bedford Square and then a college for women, at Hitchin, and finally Girton, which was to become a college of Cambridge University.

On the death of her father, Madame Bodichon (as Barbara became after her marriage to a French scientist) inherited a fortune, part of which she used to build a cottage on the Scalands Farm Estate in Sussex. She used to invite her friends who worked for the advancement of women, to come there and be 'untired', as she put it. Among these friends were George Eliot, Adelaide A. Proctor (author of *The Lost Chord*), Elizabeth Garrett Anderson, Bessie Parkes and Emily Davies, the last being destined to become the first mistress of Girton College. To Scalands also came artists and poets, including William Morris and his wife, Jane Burden, and Rossetti and his famous model, Lizzie Siddall. It was said that, whilst at Scalands, Rossetti and Lizzie became engaged. They were married in St. Clement's Church, Hastings. Their rustic idyll was immortalised by Rossetti in his poem *Silent Noon*:

Your hands lie idle in the long sweet grass,
Your eyes speak peace
So this winged hour is dropt from above
So clasp we to our hearts for a deathless dower
This close-companioned inarticulate hour
When two-fold silence was the song of love.

Their brief marriage ended with the tragic and mysterious death of Lizzie following the loss of her baby.

Some years later Rossetti again came to Sussex with another of his models, Jane Morris. His intention was to complete his picture, *Astarte or the Syrian Venus*, but the magnet which drew him was really the strange fascination exerted on him by William Blake, another artist-poet. Rossetti had the mystical idea that, at the moment he was conceived, Blake had died and his spirit had found a resting place in Rossetti's own soul. Thus, when he rented Aldwick Manor, near Bognor Regis, he felt he was treading in the steps of his twin soul. (Blake had lived in Felpham, near Bognor Regis.)

After renting a cottage for almost three years (from the landlord of the nearby Fox Inn), Blake had written to his patron, Hayley, that he was 'eternally indebted to Felpham for my three years rest from perturbation and the strength I now enjoy'. And, in verses addressed to Anna Flaxman, the wife of the sculptor, he wrote:

Away to sweet Felpham for heaven is there
The ladder of Angels descends through the air.

Unfortunately, Rossetti's stay in Aldwick Manor was ill-fated. The stormiest autumn for eighteen years aroused in him the paranoid suspicion that he was the subject of fate's malevolence. The wind uprooted an elm tree in the garden and sent draughts flying through the rooms. The shaking of the unseasonable muslin curtains made Rossetti feel 'like a ballet girl waiting in the wings'. That was the last time Jane and he were to be together for, according to another of Jane's lovers, Wilfrid Scawen Blunt, the sight of rows upon rows of empty chloral bottles and their effect on her two children ended their affair. It must have seemed to Rossetti that his soul-mate, Blake, had somehow let him down. More probably it was because (according to Blunt's boast) Jane had found in him a better and more practised lover than she did in Rossetti.

* * * * *

No account of writers in Sussex would be complete without the inclusion of Hilaire Belloc and Wilfrid Scawen Blunt. Blunt was incensed, however, when an anthology of Sussex verse (entitled *A Petworth Posie*) was published, as it included along with his own work, contributions from Hilaire Belloc and Rudyard Kipling, neither of whom was Sussex-born. Although Kipling was born in India and Belloc in France, both had become 'sons of Sussex' by adoption of that county.

In 1870 Belloc's mother had fled from France through fear of the German invaders - she, with her two children, caught the last train out of Paris for Dieppe and England. A fellow refugee was a young diplomat from the British Embassy in Paris, Wilfrid Blunt. Belloc and Blunt were both to settle in Sussex only a few miles apart and later became regular visitors to each other's homes: Blunt at

Newbuildings Place near Southwater, Belloc at Kingsland, Shipley. But before the purchase of King's Land, Belloc, as a child, had lived in several Sussex villages, mostly in Slindon.

After the flight from Paris, Madame Belloc lived for a while in Great College Street, London, but finding that the London climate with its fogs and river did not suit her boy's health, she brought the children to Sussex with their nurse, Sarah Mew. There they rented an old farm in Slindon known as Newlands, the former home of the famous cricketing brothers Newland which she re-named The Grange. Finding this home inconvenient, she moved to Slindon Cottage, close to Slindon Park, which she rented for one hundred and twenty pounds a year, and, in her old age, to another lovely cottage, Gassons, opposite the Newburgh Arms. The original choice of Slindon had been prompted by her friendship with Lady Mary Fullerton, Countess of Newburgh.

It was during Hilaire's childhood that the loss of the frigate, *Eurydice* (which went down off the Isle of Wight), prompted him to put the tragic story into verse, helped by his nurse, who set it down as he dictated.

Following Belloc's marriage to an American girl, Elodie Hogan, he brought her and their children to Courtlands, near Slindon. There he kept two pigs known as Ruskin and Carlyle, a horse named Monster, nine hens and two cocks. Later, in the village of Shipley, he bought Kingsland and its adjoining windmill which is now preserved as his memorial.

At Balliol College, Oxford, Belloc had read history and his more substantial work appears in the biographical essays he wrote on historical

Hilaire Belloc's Mill.

characters, especially those associated with the French Revolution - Marie Antoinette, Mirabeau, Danton, Fayette, Marat etc. But he first came to public notice through the ability to compose 'nonsense poems' for children, which were published as *The Bad Child's Book of Beasts*.

But Belloc's chief love was always given to his adopted homeland, the county of Sussex, and to its people. Thus in his poem, *The South Country*, he wrote somewhat nostalgically:

The great hills of the South Country
They stand along the sea;
And it's there, walking in the high woods
That I could wish to be,
And the men that were boys, when I was a boy
Walking along with me.

Belloc may have been an 'incomer' and half a foreigner, but no poet ever loved the county more than he did nor wrote of it with greater beauty of thought and words.

W. S. Blunt was born and bred in the county where his family had long been landowners and he shared his love of Sussex and his friendship with this immigrant from France, Hilaire Belloc. Blunt's love was for the Weald and on his tomb in the woods behind Newbuildings Place are to be found his words in praise of it from *Chanclebury Ring*:

Dear checker-work of woods the Sussex Weald!
If a name thrills me yet of things of earth,
That name is thine. How often I have fled
To thy deep hedgerows and embraced each field,
Each lag, each pasture, - fields which gave me birth
And saw my youth, and which must hold me dead.

Belloc was a devout Catholic who went to mass every day and 'told his beads' every morning; Blunt, a lapsed Catholic, inclined to Islam so that at his funeral, it was alleged, excerpts were read from the Bible and from the Koran. Belloc delighted in fine wines but Blunt was a near teetotaller. Belloc had but one great love in his life, Elodie Hogan, the wife whose death he mourned for twenty-three years; Blunt was a notorious amorist and careful to choose his lovers from among his social equals, preferably his kinsfolk, yet these two poets and Sussex landowners were accustomed to dine together each Sunday when they were at home in Sussex.

It is doubtful if Blunt ever walked when he could ride or drive. He used to travel miles across England driving two Arab horses harnessed in tandem to his high-wheeled dogcart.

Hilaire Belloc delighted in the taking of long walks and in fact celebrated the Queen's Jubilee of 1897 by participating in, and breaking the record for, the walk of one hundred and seventy-one miles from Oxford to York. His enthusiasm initiated the walk now known as the South Downs Way which stretches from Beachy Head to near Petersfield, some eighty miles.

Belloc also walked from Toul (his old garrison town in France) to Rome, described in the *Path to Rome*, perhaps his masterpiece, written in 1902, and in the Pyrenees which inspired his famous poem which begins: 'Do you remember an inn, Miranda'. (The poem refers not to a lady but to one of the Dukes of Miranda who accompanied Belloc.)

But perhaps Belloc's most notable walk was that which inspired *The Four Men*. Subtitled *A Farrago* - in other words, 'a confused mass', it records a walk he made from 'The George' at Robertsbridge to South Harting at the foot of the scarp far to the west. It is unlikely that four men ever made the walk because it is generally assumed that the three characters who accompanied the narrator (Belloc himself), the philosophic Grizzlebeard, the Sailor and the Poet, are all elements of his own personality. The walk has recently been relived in a delightful book by Bob Copper, a writer who also deserves a place in the literature of Sussex.

Raised on a farm in Rottingdean, where his father was bailiff, Bob first chronicled a century of Downland farming in *A Song for Every Season*, linking it with the folk-songs passed down through the years and for which he and his family have earned an international reputation. He continued the sequence with *Songs and Southern Breezes* and then described his boyhood in *Early to Rise*. All evoke a pattern of life which has long since disappeared and which, happily, he has recaptured so beautifully.

In his young days Bob Copper got to know another Sussex writer whose reputation has been revitalised recently. Barclay Wills, whose passion for natural history saved him from the frustrations of suburban life, came to Sussex soon after the Great War. He tried to run a café in Dyke Road, Brighton, and failed equally when he took up grocery in Worthing because he was absent from business much of the time communing with his beloved Downs. His great interest lay with the lives of the shepherds and the great flocks they seemed to control so effortlessly. He wrote of them in three charming books, an anthology of which was published in 1989, illustrated by Gordon Benningfield.

Several other great writers have found their inspiration in hill and vale, creek and cliff. Among the most notable are Richard Jefferies, W. H. Hudson and Tickner Edwardes. The first two share a last resting place in Broadwater Cemetery in Worthing.

Richard Jefferies was a naturalist who spent the last few years of his short life in the Sussex he had come to love. His fondness of the countryside translated into brilliant descriptive writing. The final chapters of *Nature near London* are entitled *To Brighton*, *The Southdown Shepherd*, and *The Breeze on Beachy Head*. In the first of these he sees the rail journey to the coast with an eye to the wildlife along the line, before reaching the destination - a town which he much admired, not only for its architecture but also for the ever-changing parade of colourful people who came there. The second chapter observes the lonely life of the shepherd intent only on his flock and his faithful collie, while the third is a classic portrait of the great chalk cliff and the distilled breezes which caress its inland slopes.

W. H. Hudson, having spent nearly thirty years on the pampas of the Argentine, came to Southern England with a fresh eye. *Nature in Downland* witnessed his acute observation of plant life and its interdependent insects and birds. He helped a generation to appreciate the majesty of the great, rolling, open hills and the ever-changing skyscapes above. Remarkably, he wrote the first chapter in the house in Goring in which Richard Jeffries had died. When searching for it he was startled by an apparition of a tramp he recognised immediately, from portraits, as his predecessor. Hudson was haunted by the anguished face he saw. Around the kerb of the grave in which he and his wife Emily are buried is a fitting tribute:-

'He loved birds and green places and the wind on the heath, and he saw the brightness of the skirts of God'.

*   *   *   *   *

The county of Sussex nearly earned the distinction of having given to England three of her Poets Laureate.

One who had that honour conferred on him was Alfred Lord Tennyson. In 1868 he built a house for himself on the slopes of Blackdown overlooking the western Weald, near Haslemere, and named it Aldworth. There were many of his admirers who wished to make it a place of pilgrimage but were to be disappointed, for Tennyson did not welcome visitors to his retreat. According to Kipling, the day came when a group of bedraggled, down-at-heel men called and when he demanded to know who they were, they replied: 'The last of the Light Brigade, Sir'. The heroes whose exploits he had celebrated were now the forgotten men of an ungrateful nation, content to leave to the streets and the workhouse the charge of the Light Brigade.

Either of two other Sussex poets might have succeeded Tennyson in the Laureateship; one was Rudyard Kipling, but he refused it as he did all honours which were remotely political in origin. The other, Alice Meynell, might easily have made literary history for, had she been elected, she would have been the first woman Poet Laureate. However, she was passed over in favour of Robert Bridges.

The Meynells, Alice and her husband Wilfred, lived at Humphrey's Homestead, near Greatham, and their home was a meeting place for some of the most important literary figures of the day. At least three English poets professed themselves in love with this beautiful and gifted lady - Tennyson, G. K. Chesterton and poor little Francis Thompson who declared that Mrs. Meynell was as beautiful as any of the poems she had written. Kipling also admired her poetry and loved to read it aloud in his melodious voice.

At the age of twenty-one Alice had converted to Roman Catholicism but had the misfortune to fall in love with her instructor in the faith, Father Dignam, S. J. In her poem, *Renunciation,* she gave expression to the first, though not the last, great grief of her life.

Mrs. Meynell and her husband had been instrumental in rescuing Francis Thompson from utter destitution and had been the first to recognise his latent genius. It was through their influence that he was put in the care of the Storrington monks and cured, to some extent, of his addiction to drugs. They also enlisted Blunt's interest and practical sympathy - he lent the poet a cottage, called Rascals, on his estate and arranged for Thompson to visit Newbuildings Place each day. A few weeks after his last visit Thompson died, but not before he had bequeathed to posterity some perfect pearls of poetry. Some of these, such as *Ode to the Setting Sun* were begun in the Field of the Cross at Storrington Priory whilst his lovely tribute to childhood, *Daisy,* with its lines:

The hills look over on the South
And southward dreams the sea
And with the sea-breeze, hand in hand
Came innocence and she.
O there were flowers in Storrington
On the turf and on the spray
But the sweetest flower on the Sussex hills
Was the Daisy flower, that day.

owes its inspiration to the time he spent in Sussex.

Alice Meynell had a sister, Elizabeth (always known as Minnie). She was an artist whose subjects were drawn mainly from battle scenes. As she was married to an army officer, General Sir William Francis Butler, this is not surprising. Some of her paintings were set in Sussex and when she searched for a setting for Tennyson's famous Valley of Hell for *The Charge of the Light Brigade*, she found it in Findon Valley. Today, the Russian cannon which volleyed and thundered have been replaced by sedate bungalows and villas.

* * * * *

One of the most prolific of lady novelists, who set her stories in the county, was Sheila Kaye-Smith. Born in 1887, the daughter of a Hastings doctor, she was obsessed with writing novelettes whilst at school. The self-imposed training bore fruit when she was only twenty-one and *The Tramping Methodist* was published. Her early novels sold only in small numbers but she persisted and before long she enjoyed a wider readership with *Green Apple Harvest* and *Joanna Godden*. All the tales, and there were many, were set in the varied countryside of East Sussex and Romney Marsh. She was able to convey her real love of the wide open skies above the marsh and of the sheltered farms in ancient valleys, inland from Hastings. Ever drawn to Catholicism, she was eventually received into the Church. First she built an oratory at her home, Little Doucegrove, near Northiam, and then, in 1935, a church on her own land. Sheila Kaye-Smith died in 1956 but her spirit lives on in the characters she created.

* * * * *

Most artists need patrons and both Blake and Romney found one in William Hayley of Eartham House. He was, in those days, an acceptable poet, famous for his epitaphs and also a writer of biography. It was as the illustrator of Hayley's *Life of William Cowper* that Blake came to work at Felpham.

Hayley was a wealthy though somewhat eccentric character. He insisted on wearing cavalry-type spurs when he rode and, in inclement weather, carried one of the newfangled umbrellas while on horseback. He had twice married without issue but had a son by his housekeeper. Unhappily, the boy suffered from curvature of the spine and died young, much to his father's sorrow.

Among Hayley's works was a long poem entitled *The Triumph of Temper*. It taught young ladies that the reward of a good husband was more likely to come to those who never allowed the irritability of parents and relations to upset them. Parents were naturally delighted and the work began to find a place on every parlour table; it ran to twelve editions. It was said that Hayley reflected the tastes of his day because his own was not superior to it. He was a good-hearted man of whom the poet Southey said: 'Everything about the man was good except his poetry'.

The last verses Hayley composed were not devoid of merit; they ran:

Ye gentle birds that perch aloof,
And smooth your pinions on my roof,
Preparing for departure hence,
E'er winter's angry threats commence,
Like you, my soul would smooth her plume
For longer flights beyond the tomb.

The artist, Romney, a frequent visitor to Eartham, did the illustrations for Hayley's *Triumphs of Temper*. The author also wrote *The Story of Serena,* and the model for some of Romney's plates was none other than Emma Hart, before she became Lady Hamilton. She is said to have admired the sentiments of the poem though, according to her lover, Charles Greville, she herself possessed an ungovernable temper.

Hayley built himself a house to his own designs, down in Felpham and let Eartham House to William Huskisson M.P., a gentleman who, through his own folly, had the singular distinction of being the first individual to be killed by a railway engine. This tragic event occurred at the opening of the Manchester - Liverpool Railway in 1830. George Stephenson, of *Rocket* fame, had told Huskisson to stay in his carriage and not to get down on to the railway line. He disregarded this instruction and was killed by a passing engine.

Today Hayley, though popular in his own time, is almost forgotten. He was no doubt a better man than he was a poet. His epitaph was written by Mrs. Amelia Opie, a lady novelist, who also enjoyed the hospitality of Eartham House. She wrote of her deceased friend: 'He concluded a life of kindness with a death of peace'.'

*　*　*　*　*

In the summer of 1894 there came to Worthing the author of what has come to be regarded as one of the most famous lines in English drama - 'A handbag!!' which quotation is, of course, found in Oscar Wilde's witty comedy *The Importance of being Earnest.* It was written whilst Wilde, his wife and his two sons were on holiday in Worthing and staying at The Haven, 5 Esplanade, a building now replaced by a large block of flats.

The idea for this comedy seems to have originated at King's Cross Station where a hamper left in the goods department was found to contain a baby about two weeks old, wrapped in wadding, together with its feeding bottle. The baby was taken to the police station but there was no trace of the man who had left the hamper.

Wilde would have read the item in the *Worthing Gazette* and transferred the incident from King's Cross Station to Victoria, whilst the hamper became a handbag. Another item in the *Gazette* about the same time reported the death of a Captain Bunbury, a name he used in his play along with the character named John Worthing (Ernest). In a letter to Lord Alfred Douglas he wrote: 'I have been doing nothing but bathing and playwriting. My play is really very funny. I am quite delighted with it, but it is not shaped yet. It lies in Sibylline leaves about the room and Arthur (the butler) has twice made a chaos of it by tidying up. The result, however, was rather dramatic. I am inclined to think the chaos is a stronger evidence for an Intelligent Creator than Cosmos is. The view might be expanded'. To another friend he wrote: 'I am in a very much worse state for money than I told you, but I am finishing a new play which, as it is quite nonsensical and has no serious interest, will I hope bring me in a lot of gold'.

In a letter to W. B. Yeats, who was at the time compiling *A Book of Irish Verse* (to be published in 1895), he wrote: 'I have just finished a play so my handwriting is abominable'.

Whilst he was in Worthing a Water Carnival was held, with the public voting on the best decorated boats. In the evening Wilde presented the prizes at the Pier Pavilion and proceeded to congratulate Worthing on the town's beauty and amenities, including the lovely long walks which he recommended to other people but admitted he didn't take himself. He also spoke of the town's excellent water supply and said he had been told that total abstainers who visited Worthing were so struck with the purity and excellence of the water that they only wished everybody would drink nothing else. Worthing would have been glad of this commendation as, some twenty years earlier, sewage from a storage tank had contaminated the nearby waterworks in Little High Street and led to an epidemic of typhoid fever in which many died. Such a tragedy had done nothing to enhance the resort's popularity at the time. Wilde, having regard to the fashion of the age, commended Worthing on its facility of offering pleasure! He held that whenever a person was happy he was good although, perhaps, when he was good he was not always happy! There was no excuse for anyone not being happy in such surroundings. This was his first visit but would not be his last, he said.

The play so closely identified with Worthing had its first performance at St. James's Theatre, London the following February, some five months after being written and ever since has occupied an honourable place in theatrical repertoire.

There can be few who, in an indirect way, have done more for English literature than the one-time occupant of St. George's Lodge, Worthing, William Ernest Henley who lived there from 1899-1901.

This was not because he was a poetic genius, though he did write poetry, nor because he was a literary critic who edited and originated a sixpenny monthly journal, *The Scottish Observer*, which was 'the focus of more concentrated promise and brilliance than any other sixpennyworth of the age'. It was because he was quick to recognise genius in others and to encourage and promote it. Thus it was that Henley identified the latent promise of a string of future writers of distinction including Hardy, Wells, Barrie, Stevenson, Yeats, Conrad and Kipling and a music critic, the Irishman G. B. Shaw. The early work of these men first saw the light of day in the journals of which W. E. Henley was the editor. He has been described by Denis Thirkell as tall, bearded and burly, and according to J. M. Barrie in *Sentimental Tommy*, 'his beard licked the table as he wrote'. To some of his biographers he was arrogant, short-tempered and contemptuous. Small wonder, as from his youth he was haunted by illness. At an early age he had a tubercular foot which had to be amputated so that he walked with a wooden leg and a crutch.

Those who read Henley's life story are impressed by the courage which marked his progress. His poem *Invictus* gives an unexaggerated description of the author. His masterfulness and defiance of physical limitations led Robert Louis Stevenson, with whom he had become acquainted in an Edinburgh hospital, to use him as a model for Long John Silver in *Treasure Island*. It was only in the closing years of his life, when living in Worthing, that his unconquerable spirit seems to have dropped 'in the fell clutch of circumstance', so that, as he wrote in his poem, *Hawthorn and Lavender*, of Shoreham's River Adur and a rotting hulk stranded in the mud, he dropped his guard and exclaimed: 'Good God, it's I'.

Apart from his physical handicaps Henley, like Rudyard Kipling, suffered deep sorrow through the loss of an adored little daughter. Her name was Margaret and she died in 1894 when only five years old. During his earlier years the family had lived in Battersea and were often visited by the young men who belonged to what the wags called 'The Henley Regatta', although to be known as one of Henley's young men was accounted an accolade. Among them was J. M. Barrie who was enchanted by little Margaret whom he recalled in his book *The Greenwood Hat*. This tells of an earlier time in Edinburgh when he first met her, and describes her sitting on her father's knee as he played the piano, or dancing gaily round the room. Later in Battersea she would call him 'Friendy' or 'Friendy Wendy' and when he came to write *Peter Pan* he remembered the name first coined by the little girl. Since then lots of little girls have been called Wendy though it is doubtful if many have known that their name originated with a child whose Daddy once lived in Worthing; nor do those who read *Treasure Island* realise that the person who was the inspiration for the notorious Long John Silver occupied, for a few years, St. George's Lodge at the junction of Ladydell and Chesswood Roads in that town.

The lodge is an elegant Victorian villa where a spare room was always kept for his visitors, some of whom had been included in the celebrated 'Henley Regatta'. Henley used to sit under the splendid portico of his home and, whilst watching the sunset, might have written his elegiac poem *Margaritae Sorori* (translated as *Margaret, little playmate*), the last verse of which runs:

So be my passing!
My task accomplish'd and the long day done,
My wages taken, and in my heart
Some late lark singing,
Let me be gather'd to the quiet west,
The sundown splendid and serene,
Death.

After his daughter died, Henley gave Josephine Kipling (Rudyard's eldest child) Margaret's silver porringer and when Rudyard died in the Middlesex Hospital in 1936, years after his daughter's death, his wife Carrie presented the porringer to that hospital (where it might possibly still be gathering dust in some cupboard). It was a sad memorial of two fathers bound together by a love of literature and a shared grief. Rudyard's only allusion to the loss of Josephine, his little daughter, are in the poem *Merrow Down* and in a short story with the obscure title *They*, whilst Margaret Henley is immortalised as Wendy in Barrie's *Peter Pan*.

* * * * *

Towards the end of the nineteenth century a new star appeared on the British literary horizon: Henry Rider Haggard, whose novels of adventure in the 'dark continent' (as Africa was known) soon became bestsellers and set families (including the Kiplings) squabbling over who should have 'the first read' of the latest publication. In 1886 came *King Solomon's Mines* to be followed by *She* and *Allan Quatermain*. The popularity of these novels was such that critics and writers were provoked (possibly by envy) into hoping for the day to dawn when

The Rudyards cease from Kipling
And the Haggards ride no more.

Rider Haggard owned an estate in Norfolk where he had a model farm; he became an authority on advanced farming methods and was knighted for his services to agriculture. He also owned a seaside residence in Sussex in the new suburb of St. Leonard's, Hastings. He and Kipling became close friends and Haggard was a regular visitor at Bateman's where he became one of the privileged few who were invited into the study, where the two men were known to develop plots for stories. These conversations in the study and at table were wont to continue well into the night, long after the cook and parlour maid had hoped to clear away. On at least one occasion the servants hurried the proceedings by sprinkling pepper on the serving hatch and wafting it gently into the room. Haggard began to sneeze and, suspecting the onset of a cold, Kipling packed him off to bed, much to the relief of the staff who were eager to retire to their own quarters in the converted oast-house.

Like Kipling and Henley, Haggard suffered the loss of a young child - his son, Arthur, and always regretted the fact that he was away in South America when the boy died. He was there to search for Montezuma's treasure and collect specimens of local flora. Haggard had left Arthur (always known as Jock) in the care of a fellow critic, Edmund Gosse, and the boy had caught measles; this was followed by a perforated ulcer from which he died. Haggard was haunted by guilt, as Kipling may well have been regarding his daughter Josephine. Against advice, Kipling had taken his family to New York to contest American copyright theft. After the worst crossing of the Atlantic they had ever experienced, during which the children and their nurse were wracked with seasickness, they arrived in New York to face the rigours of the winter. The children contracted whooping cough and Josephine, while being in the care of the Forest family in Long Island, did not regain strength and died. Something in her father died with her.

Thus the Kipling daughter and the Haggard son both died while their fathers were involved in the pursuit of money. Haggard recognised this and admitted it. He had gone to Mexico with the presentiment that he and the boy should not meet again in this world, but he had presumed that he himself would not survive the expedition. Despite this, he had gone in search of gold in Mexico and the boy had died. He was torn by unbearable feelings of loss and guilt. He felt that he should have read the signs and presentiments more clearly. He brooded over his loss for the rest of his days. Nobody was allowed to speak of Jock and a cloud of sorrow darkened the Norfolk home, relieved only when a daughter, Lilias, was born in 1893.

It was at Bateman's that he renewed his acquaintance with Kipling's friend, Colonel Wemyss Feilden, who recalled how, hearing of Jock's birth, he and a friend had ridden twenty-seven miles to welcome the first white baby to be born in Zululand.

*　*　*　*　*

Thomas Hardy is best remembered for his novels and poems, but as a youth he trained as an architect. This was at a time when considerable church building or restoration was the order of the day and Hardy served his apprenticeship with a distinguished church architect of London.

He was William Arthur Bloomfield, son of Charles James Bloomfield, who was the Bishop of London, and it was probably a combination of business and pleasure that brought young Hardy to Sussex in the year 1866. At the time his employer was engaged in the building of three churches in the county - St. Luke's in Brighton, St. John's in Preston, near Brighton, and St. Andrew's in Victoria Road, Worthing. Bloomfield was also asked by Lord Montague to carry out alterations to Easebourne Church. According to Millgate, in his book about Thomas Hardy, it was a case of *cherchez la femme* that brought Hardy to Findon - Elizabeth Nicoll, daughter of the landlord of the Running Horse, Nepcote, being the lady in question.

According to the definitive biography of Hardy, not only did he pay a visit to Findon but he also sketched the little Gothic Church of St. John the Baptist.

St. Andrew's, Worthing, was a product of the Tractarian Movement within the Church of England, originally inspired by men like Newman, Pusey, Keble and Manning as they sought to recall the national Church to its origins in the Church of Rome. In Worthing, two people who were in sympathy with the revival and the form it took were Sir Robert and Lady Loder, of Beach House, who contributed liberally to the building fund. In 1897, twelve years after the building of St. Andrew's, Lady Loder followed the example of Newman and Manning and many others who rejoined the Roman Catholic communion during those years.

Two members of an extraordinary family have left an indelible impression on the attractive hill-top town Rye. Originally an island port, a member of the Confederation of the Cinque Ports, and based firmly in the maritime history of England, it has long since lost most of its water to inexorable coastal deposition, but it still retains a charm reflecting its past. A number of artists and writers have succumbed to its atmosphere, Edward Burra and Paul Nash, Henry James, Radclyffe Hall, Rumer Godden, and Esther Meynell, but A. C. and E. F. Benson are also very much part of so unusual a coterie. Their dominant father, E. W. Benson, was Archbishop of Canterbury, and they and their brother Hugh and sister Maggie formed a strange quartet. A privileged background gave ample opportunity for them to pursue their own interests. Both Arthur (A. C.) and Fred (E. F.) wrote, the former an autobiographical account which ran to four million words, and the latter about a hundred books, mostly novels, which reflected the social life of the well-to-do. Arthur, a don, and subsequently Master of Magdelene College, Cambridge, shared Lamb House in Rye, he in the vacations and Fred during University terms. Fred loved Rye and immortalised the little town and its social life as 'Tilling' in four of his six Mapp and Lucia novels. His descriptions of the cobbled streets and elegant houses in which the comedy of manners is set are a delight. Lamb House is cast as 'Mallards' the home of the snobbish and inquisitive Miss Elizabeth Mapp who reigned supreme in 'Tilling' before the advent of the pretentious Emmeline Lucas and her consort, Georgie Pilson. Other supporting characters are equally sharply but slightly overdrawn and were almost certainly based on various Rye personalities.

E. F. Benson was, much to his surprise, elected Mayor of Rye in 1934, an unusual honour for a non-councillor, and was twice re-elected. His wealth enabled him to be a benefactor to the community. Among his gifts were the stained glass windows used to beautify the great church of St. Mary the virgin which crowns the hill-top. The first, in 1928, with the help of his brother's patron, was to commemorate his brother Arthur. The Benedicite Window dominates the South Transept and is filled with medallions containing the *Omnia Opera* - everything on earth and in sky and in sea which praises the Lord. It is modelled in the style of the windows of Chartres, but in it is set Arthur, in the robes of his Mastership. It features also a mountain in Cumberland, which for some unexplained reason Arthur owned, as well as the likeness of his father, the Archbishop. This was followed, in 1937, by the West Window, dedicated to the memory of his parents. A host of angels fill the upper section, an idea which came to him when sitting in his Secret Garden just before the Christmas of 1936, when a dazzling white seagull flew behind the tracery of the branches of a pear tree. He saw in his imagination angels among the leaded divisions of a stained glass window. They were destined to fly over a Nativity scene. Among the attendant sheep are featured Fred's beloved collie, Taffy, and his devoted manservant , Charlie Tomlin, dressed as the shepherd. In the right hand corner is Benson himself in

Lamb House

The Mermaid Inn, Rye.

Rye

The Cuckmere Valley.

Mayoral regalia. It would not be easy, in these days, for anyone to make so discreet a memorial. Fred Benson died in February 1940, a few months before a stray German bomb demolished the Garden Room which was such a distinguished feature of Lamb House. He took Rye to his heart and Rye, surely, thought very highly of him.

Some writers will for ever be associated with a particular part of the Sussex countryside. Tickner Edwardes with the Burpham of *'Tansy'* and *'Neighbourhood'*; Michael Fairless, the pseudonym of Margaret Fairless Barber, with the inner Adur valley around Shermanbury - her *'Roadmender'* country, and Barclay Wills with the Downs. Dirk Bogarde has however made a significant and glorious mark writing about that lovely valley of the Cuckmere in which he spent many youthful holidays. His father, the chief photographer of *The Times* bought a house just across the river from Alfriston. The magical days spent by the young Dirk were wonderfully re-created in his first volume of his autobiography *A Postillion Struck By Lightning*. It is full of interest for the lover of Sussex and conveys the atmosphere of the early 1930's. His boyhood activities, much in company with his sister and their nanny - 'Lally' - are crystallised with a clarity which speaks volumes for a marvellous memory and a skill with words. An episode when he and his friends, Reg and Perce, were disturbed whilst fishing in the river is masterly. The lady who was described by Perce as 'They do say she's a bit do-lally-lap', was Virginia Woolf, who had wandered over from Charleston Farmhouse, but seemed to have no sense of direction. He contributed 'Windover Hill' to an anthology of Britain and his impression of the passing seasons as they affected the landscape seen from above the Long Man of Wilmington, an enigmatic chalk-figure couched in the coombe of the hill, is quite breath-taking. More recently, in 1992, he produced *Great Meadow*. Subtitled 'An Evocation' it is dedicated to the faithful Lally, and is an account of life in the valley seen through the eyes of, and with the limited vocabulary of, a young boy. It lives up to its subtitle for he recalls a way of life which has disappeared with the onset of war. One can almost hear the sounds and smell the scents of bus-travel, of seaside adventures and of harvest times so long ago.

Many others have added their own particular love of Sussex in a variety of ways. Fortunately by browsing among the overloaded shelves of second hand book shops we can join them in their passion. The guides, like E. V. Lucas, Esther Meynell and Arthur Becket, the interpreters of landscape and its mysteries like Donald Maxwell, Thurston Hopkins and Hadrian Allcroft want to share their deeply won knowledge. Naturalists and countrymen, poets and philosophers have also been attracted to our varied scenes; novelists have set countless tales in the county and autobiographical memories are constantly being discovered anew. One of the most charming is the childhood happiness recounted by Angela Thirkell in and around Rottingdean. In *Three Houses* she describes visits to her grandparents' home, North End House and the enjoyment of simple pleasures with her cousins Josephine and Elsie

Kipling. Again it is sharp observation which brings into focus the fun to be had on the beach, in the shops in the High Street, in the gentle Downs and of the villagers who were such characters. The richness of the legacy of Sussex literature must be virtually unrivalled in Britain and it is still there for us to discover if only we take the trouble to do so.

'The Down Countree'

'The White Chalk Coast'

William Juxon, Archbishop of Canterbury.
Reproduced by kind permission of the Church Commissioners: photograph
Courtauld Institute of Art.

VII   PRELATES AND PRINCES OF THE CHURCH

Sussex folk have been inclined, through the centuries, to be stubbornly Protestant yet the comparative remoteness of the county, its Downs, thick forests, and its roads (which, before macadam, were at times nigh impassable) have led to its becoming a place of refuge for the adherents of what was called the 'old faith' - Roman Catholicism. Not surprisingly, out of this devoted nucleus have come several priests, at least two of whom were destined to become cardinals, princes of the Church.

The village of Henfield has been described (somewhat unfairly) as being famous for nothing else but the birthplace of Thomas Stapleton and, in his *Worthies of Sussex*, Thomas Fuller, the seventeenth-century biographer, relates that Stapleton was born 'in the same year and month wherein Sir Thomas Moore was beheaded, as if divine providence had purposely dropped from heaven an acorn in place of the oak that was felled'. Thomas Moore lost his head through his refusal to acknowledge Henry VIII as 'supreme Head on earth of the Church of England'. For the sake of like principles Thomas Stapleton spent many years in exile.

His father was in the service of the Bishop of Chichester as a steward or agent and the boy grew up at Drayton Manor near Oving, West Sussex. About one hundred and twenty years after his death it was claimed that his birthplace was Henfield. He entered the priesthood after being educated at Winchester and New College, Oxford. By the age of twenty-three he was a prebendary of Chichester but, on the accession of Elizabeth, removed to Louvain where he studied theology. On his return to England in 1563 he was deprived of his prebend through his refusal to deny the authority of the Pope. He returned to Louvain and engaged with William Allen (later Cardinal Allen) in the founding of the English College at Douai. The aims of this college were to prepare a company of missionary priests for the reconversion of England.

Stapleton became an erudite and skilful controversialist on behalf of his Church and, although he spent the rest of his life in exile, never forgot the place of his birth. He used to sign himself, Didymus, the Truth-Teacher of Henfield *(Didymus Veredicus Henfildanus)*, Didymus being the nickname of the apostle Thomas.

He is described, rather quaintly, by Fuller, as 'a man of mild demeanour and unsuspected integrity' - a somewhat ambiguous description. 'In strictness of life', wrote Fuller, 'he equalled Cardinal Allen and in gentility, exceeded him and in painfulness of writing on behalf of the Romish Church his ability was drowned in Allen's activity'.

Philip of Spain appointed him Professor of Scripture at Louvain; he became Master of a College there and was, for forty years, *Dominus ad oppositum* - Undertaker-General against the Protestant heresy.

It became customary to ship the priests he had trained to Shoreham-by-Sea, Sussex. From there, often disguised as labourers, they slipped up the River Adur and came to West Grinstead. The presbytery there became a dispersal point for the missionaries. Numbers of them were apprehended and brutally martyred and, in the presbytery, there is preserved a letter from one of them, Father Francis Bell, who died at Tyburn in 1643. The priest's house at West Grinstead contains a secret chapel in the roof and could well be the oldest presbytery in England.

Thomas Stapleton was offered a reward for his labours in the form of a Cardinal's Hat but the offer came too late. Frailty of body prevented him from undertaking the journey from Louvain to Rome and he died shortly afterwards: he was buried in St. Peter's, Louvain.

In the year 1887, a young priest moved from Mortlake to West Grinstead to serve as curate to the Very Rev. Mgr. John Baptist Denis, founder of the Roman Catholic Church of Our Lady of Consolation - the name of the young priest was the Rev. Francis Bourne.

He spent only two years in West Sussex, but during that time he commenced a seminary in the priest's house where the first students of the Roman Catholic Diocese of Southwark began their training for the priesthood. In 1889, Father Bourne rented a white-washed farmhouse in Henfield in which to continue his work and, in 1891, this moved to Surrey and became Wonersh Seminary.

Before he became a teacher, Francis had undergone a long period of training at St. Cuthbert's College, Ushaw, St. Edmund's, Ware, Saint-Sulpice, Paris and the University of Louvain. He was well equipped to teach others.

Subsequently he became Bishop of the Southwark Roman Catholic Diocese and, in 1903, was instituted Archbishop of Westminster. Eight years later he received his Cardinal's Hat.

Francis Bourne was not only a scholar; he was endowed with considerable administrative and diplomatic skills. At the Eucharistic Congress of 1908, he contrived to gain permission for a visit by the Papal Legate, the first time this had been permitted since the days of Cardinal Reginald Pole. He had come to England as Papal Legate in 1554; two years later Pole was made Archbishop of Canterbury and, during the reign of Mary Tudor, was considered as having the primary responsibility for the death of many Protestants. To have gained permission for another Papal Legate to come to Protestant England - fed for years on John Foxe's *Book of Martyrs* - suggests considerable skill in the arts of diplomacy. Created cardinal in 1911 he died in 1935.

Another future cardinal of the Roman Catholic Church commenced his clerical life as a priest of the Church of England. His name was Henry Edward Manning, at one time a leader of the Tractarian

Movement at the beginning of the nineteenth century. After J. H. Newman's secession, he was regarded as one of the leaders of the 'Oxford Movement', as it came to be called.

His father, a West Indian merchant and a Governor of the Bank of England, was so proud a man that only a bishop was regarded as good enough to preside at the baptism of his son, Henry Edward. The boy was reared in an atmosphere of evangelical piety. He was educated at Dr. Hooker's school, Rottingdean, and later, at Harrow and Oxford.

At Oxford, he was a year senior to W. E. Gladstone and a year junior to Samuel Wilberforce, his future brother-in-law. He left Balliol College with the idea of entering politics but his father's bankruptcy dashed his hopes. The offer of a Merton fellowship induced him to take Holy Orders and, after ordination, Wilberforce found him a curacy with the Rev. John Sargent, Rector of Woolavington-cum-Graffham, West Sussex. He then followed Wilberforce's example and married one of the Rev. Sargent's daughters, Caroline, and subsequently became rector in the place of his deceased father-in-law. It was not long before he was appointed Archdeacon of Chichester Diocese.

But the fates were not to continue smiling on the up-and-coming clergyman. Shortly after his happy marriage, Caroline died. Manning was inconsolable and was even accustomed to writing his sermons at her grave-side. (He became known as a distinguished and eloquent preacher.)

After a time he found comfort in the friendship of the widow of Francis Blunt, an officer in the Grenadier Guards, wounded at Corunna, and a member of the Prince Regent's set. He had died from a chill, contracted whilst out cub-hunting; after four years of marriage his wife was left a widow with three children.

Mary Blunt was to be described by her son Wilfrid as 'poetical, religious, inclined to scepticism and passionate in affection'. Manning thought her the wittiest woman he had ever met and he began to ride over from Lavington to Petworth each afternoon to enjoy Mary's friendship. She, in her turn, mischievously dubbed him the 'Doctor of the Genteels': this on account of the way ambition prompted him to seek the company of well-connected and influential people. Like his father, Henry was an ambitious man and a self-confessed ambitious man too. 'I do feel pleasure', he wrote, 'in honour, precedence, elevation and the society of great people', a proclivity he was to admit as being 'very shameful and mean'. It is plain that Mary Blunt was not just witty; she was perceptive too.

Although their friendship was, according to her son Wilfrid, 'not wholly devoid of sentiment', nothing came of it and, just as in later life Manning had regarded the death of his young wife as 'one of God's special mercies' (viewed, presumably, *sub specie aeternitatis*), it may be that he saw his friendship with Mary Blunt in the same light, for on Trinity Sunday 1855 she died. Five years later Manning had resigned the living at Lavington and, a few months afterwards, entered the Roman Catholic Church.

His promotion was rapid. His High Church views, previously a handicap to advancement, now became an asset whilst his natural astuteness (which distinguished him more than saintliness and learning), made him a worthy successor to Cardinal Wolsey as a diplomatic and administrative cleric.

At the Vatican Council of 1869-1870 he strenuously supported the newly-advanced doctrine of Papal Infallibility, a doctrine which still divides the Christian Churches. He was bitterly opposed to the admission of Roman Catholics to the Universities, an attitude which alienated him from Cardinal Newman after 1866.

Six years after his secession he was made Provost of the Westminster Metropolitan Chapter and, eight years later, Roman Catholic Archbishop of Westminster. He worked for the building of Westminster Cathedral and, in 1875, received his Cardinal's Hat which 'he wore' until his death in 1892.

Although Henry Manning was never able to 'suffer fools gladly' and found difficulties in the realm of personal relationships, he exhibited a profound concern for the sufferings of the Victorian working-class man and his family. He was one of those socially sensitive priests who in those days championed the cause of the poor, the deprived and the oppressed. When William Booth addressed himself to the social problems of 'darkest England' he had the support of Manning, Head of the Roman Catholic Church in Britain. Booth's social work, and indeed his whole movement, was politically suspect but Manning declared not only that he believed the Salvation Army was doing 'what Our Lord and his apostles would do if they were in London', but that five thousand extra policemen could not fill its place in the repression of crime and disorder. Earlier on, he had backed Booth in his efforts to expose the white slave traffic, a business which involved the kidnapping of young women to be smuggled out to supply the brothels of Europe.

Manning was a strange man whose 'tight lips, cold eyes and forbidding air of cadaverous disapproval' hid an often tormented soul and 'a high, severe idea of the intrinsic excellence of virginity'. He refused the post of sub-almoner to Queen Victoria, only to torture himself with the fear that he had done so through the desire to be regarded as 'mortified and holy'. Perhaps he paid a high price for that pride of which he was painfully conscious and yet which he never quite overcame. Had he married Mary Blunt and continued as Archdeacon of Chichester, he might well have become Bishop within the Anglican fold. As a stepfather to young Wilfrid Scawen Blunt, who knows how much this influence might have directed the steps of that orphaned young man?

* * * * *

Two sons of Sussex, born in the Elizabethan Age, were to achieve eminence in the hierarchy of the Church of England, both being instituted archbishops. They were William Juxon, born 1582 in Chichester, who became Archbishop of Canterbury, and Accepted Frewen who received the See of York.

The Juxon family lived at Aldbourne Place and after St. John's College, Oxford, William rose to be the President of his college and Vice-Chancellor of the university. He enjoyed the friendship of Archbishop Laud, (described by some as King Charles' 'evil genius'), and assisted him in the revision of the university statutes. He was made Bishop of London and, in 1636, Laud persuaded the King to confer on Juxon the highest civil post in the land, that of Lord High Treasurer. This was the first time this prestigious position had been held by a clergyman since the reign of Henry VII.

In his own whimsical way, Thomas Fuller described the office of Lord High Treasurer as 'a troublesome place in those times, it being expected that he should make much brick yet with little straw allowed unto him'. Despite this handicap, Juxon seems to have been an efficient treasurer for, as Fuller continues: 'The coffers he found empty he left filling, and had left full, had peace been preserved in the land'.

Already in possession of a reputation for tolerance and integrity, and enjoying the respect of the members of various branches of Christianity, Juxon won fresh laurels and an enhanced reputation as Lord High Treasurer. 'So mild was his temper that petitioners for money, when it was not to be had, departed well pleased with his denials', and when 'few spoke well of bishops in that time, and of lord treasurers at all times, he possessed his soul in patience'.

King Charles also chose Juxon as his confessor and it was in this capacity that he attended his King on the scaffold, on that January day in 1649 when he was beheaded. His final words to the King were that he was exchanging a temporal crown for an eternal one. After the King's death, Juxon, his chaplain, was deprived of the See of London and, although he was not greatly molested during the Commonwealth, it is related that soldiers visited Aldbourne Place, Sussex, at a time when William was staying with his brother John. Not taking any chances, he disguised himself as a brick-layer and, because the soldiers stayed so long searching the house, one of the chimneys is unusually large.

It was in the year that William Juxon was made Archbishop of Canterbury that Accepted Frewen, son of the Reverend John Frewen, Rector of Northiam, East Sussex, was elevated to the Archbishopric of York. Samuel Pepys was present in the Henry VII Chapel, Westminster Abbey, on 4th October 1660, and witnessed the ceremony.

The Reverend John Frewen had been inducted to the Northiam living in 1583; of a Puritan inclination, he quickly won renown as a preacher but had a Bill of Indictment preferred against him for nonconformity. Though vindicated, this did not quell the local hostility and eventually John had to appeal to the Ecclesiastical Court, before which Robert Cresswell of Northiam was brought. It was alleged that on 26th June 1621, he 'openly railed upon Mr. Frewen, calling him old fool, old ass and old coxcombe and other irreverent and disgraceful terms'. Cresswell was excommunicated.

Puritan John had eleven children, the eldest sons being named in accordance with the Puritan fashion, Accepted and Thankful. They were followed by Stephen, John (who succeeded his father as rector), and seven others. The family first lived at Carriers until, in 1593, they moved to Church House, Northiam.

The old rector died in 1628 and thus escaped the calamitous years of the Civil War. Both Accepted Frewen and his brother Thankful were forced to seek refuge in Holland during those years. Their brother Stephen proved to be a clever 'trimmer of sails' and managed both to lend King Charles ten pounds and to supply Parliament with a month's pay for the army. Not surprisingly he made a fortune, became Master of the Skinners Company, an alderman of the City of London and owner of a splendid house in Northiam called Brickwall, together with its six hundred and fifty-two acres. During their exile the older brothers stayed with a Dutch citizen, Willem Van de Herball, and, in exchange for furs and skins, he sent Stephen the bulbs of a new flower - yellow, red and pink in colour. It was known as the tulip, which first bloomed under English skies at Goatley Manor, Northiam.

When, at the Restoration, Charles II received his own again, Accepted Frewen was rewarded for his loyalty to the monarchy with the See of York. During the Civil War he had been Master of Magdalen College when Oxford was held for the King. He had sent some of the university plate to York to raise funds to be used for the prosecution of the royal cause: also he had lent his King five hundred pounds of his own money. His reward was an archbishop's mitre. Whether he ever recovered his five hundred pounds is not known. His brother, Thankful, who had the price of one thousand pounds put on his head by Parliament for his capture, dead or alive, was rewarded by being made Secretary to the Lord Keeper of the Royal Seal.

Accepted only lived to enjoy his elevation for four years and died serenely before a triple misfortune fell upon his native land: the Great Plague of London, followed by the Fire which consumed St. Paul's and, finally, the sound of Dutch guns as they burned the English warships in the Medway. His tomb may be seen to this day beside the altar in the Lady Chapel of York Minster.

Some of his descendants are still to be found in Sussex as are the fifteenth-century buildings Carriers and Brickwall. The old rectory was burned down in the nineteenth century and replaced with a new one built on adjacent ground.

Accepted Frewen, Archbishop of York.
Reproduced by kind permission of the University of York. Photograph from
Catalogue of Portraits at Bishopthorpe Palace by John Ingamells.

Lancing College Chapel.
Reproduced by kind permission of Mr. David Nicholls.

VIII   PRIESTS, PASTORS AND PREACHERS

It is likely that during the later stages of the Roman occupation groups of Christians worshipped in Sussex, for it is almost certain that a basilica occupied the site of the beautiful and historic Holy Trinity Church at Bosham. The earliest reference to a ministry may be found in the work of the Venerable Bede. In his book, *The Ecclesiastical History of the English People,* completed in 731, he writes of holy men preaching at Bosham in the mid seventh century:

But the whole kingdom of the South Saxons was ignorant of the name and faith
of God. There was, however, a certain monk there, of the Irish nation, by the name
of Dicul, who had a very small monastery in the place which is called Boshanhamm,
a spot surrounded by woods and sea. In it were five or six brethren who served the
Lord in a life of humility and poverty. None however, of the natives of the country
cared either to imitate their life or listen to their preaching.

Sussex folk have always maintained a perverse pride in the lateness of their conversion. When Wilfrid, an unconventional northern Bishop was driven ashore in Sussex in 666 he, too, was

unsuccessful. He returned twenty years later, having been exiled again, and this time managed to establish the See of Selsey. The long, slow process of confirming the church in the land of the South Saxons had begun in earnest. Since those times, and the turbulence of the creation of a church separated from its Catholic origins, the debt of England to the rectory and the vicarage (and of Scotland to the manse) is difficult to estimate. Nor is that debt confined only to those moral and spiritual values which such places have engendered, encouraged and defended.

From the parsonage have come sailors and soldiers such as Horatio Nelson and Bernard Montgomery; scholars like Henry George Liddell who, in partnership with Robert Scott, gave classical scholarship their famous Greek lexicon. In the field of English literature, the rectory has

Holy Trinity

95

given us the Rev. Charles Kingsley, author not only of *Westward Ho!* but of novels like *Yeast* and *Alton Lock* which contained the seeds of Christian socialism. Then there have been those memorable sisters, Charlotte, Emily and Anne Brontë; also poets like John Donne and Alfred Lord Tennyson; wits like Sidney Smith and Charles L. Dodgson (Lewis Carroll); headmasters like Thomas Arnold of Rugby, H.G. Liddell of Westminster and Edward Thring of Uppingham of whom it was said that 'he really made the school'.

In view of the foregoing it is not surprising that Sussex has been the home of clerical gentlemen who have been not only true priests and pastors, but also remarkable men in many other ways. Among this company were the Palmers, father and son, who between them held the living of Sullington, West Sussex, for one hundred and two years with only a brief interregnum whilst Henry became free to succeed his father.

The Rev. George Palmer, who became a Fellow of Trinity College, Cambridge, was contemporary with the Rev. Patrick Brontë of St. John's, at a time when the Rev. Charles Simeon exerted extraordinary influence, especially on those young men who intended to take Holy Orders. Simeon's curate was Henry Martyn, senior wrangler and Smith's prizeman, who became a famous missionary. He was also Patrick Brontë's hero. Moving as they did in this circle, it would be surprising if George Palmer and Brontë had been unacquainted. Thus, when both had three daughters, christened Charlotte, Emily and Anne (in that order), one is bound to wonder whether Patrick Brontë borrowed the names from his distinguished friend or whether this is but another coincidence. At any rate, a memorial window to the three Palmer sisters is to be seen in Sullington Parish Church.

The Rev. Henry Palmer was one of those blessed people (in the eyes of future biographers) who kept a diary in which he recorded everyday events (and not without a spice of humour). For instance, he recorded how he had driven to West Wantley and found the farmer's wife 'wholesomely dirty'. She must have been troubled at allowing the rector to find her like this! The Rev. Henry regularly visited the church day-school, established in a cottage in Water Lane through the generosity of George Carew-Gibson of Sandgate House. Here he taught scripture, the catechism and arithmetic and found his 'long-division girls' dull, but had the grace to ask if he himself had not been dull at that age. On another occasion he recorded that the schoolmaster had found a more genial sphere of usefulness in a toy shop in the Edgware Road. His removal, the rector dryly observed, 'could hardly have been for the worse'. In his opinion the new schoolmaster and his wife, 'a rustic couple', were more fitted for Sullington than 'their elegant predecessors'.

Sport of various kinds interested him, not least the Crawley and Horsham hounds. On one occasion, a wet and stormy January day, 'hounds were here again in full cry under the nursery window'. On a fine April day he reported, 'a day's sport on the Downs - horses, ponies and donkeys - all the Sandgate party who dined here afterwards'.

On another occasion he reported on the despatch of his man-servant to Pulborough to exchange 'a young and pretty cook for one old and ugly'. One is bound to wonder what occasioned such an exchange; was it fortuitous or designed?

By the mid-nineteenth century, cricket was firmly established as a popular sport, and one in which members of all classes were happily joined. The Rev. George was evidently one of the great succession of cricketing parsons and reported with satisfaction that his team, Sullington, captained by one Stopford, played the 'Faithfullites' - a team picked from the forty or so young men who attended the Rev. George Faithfull's army coaching establishment in Storrington.

Not that George Palmer neglected his parochial duties. He regularly conducted three services each Sunday and took his sermon-making with the seriousness it deserved. During the week he held 'cottage lectures'. He deplored the failure of the working class to attend Sullington Church and prayed that he might have grace to bring them to a full appreciation of this great assistance on their road to heaven.

Henry Palmer, when a boy, laid the foundation stone of a new rectory (now known as the Old Rectory). The stone for the new building was quarried from the ground where the new churchyard stands. In 1938 the rectory was deemed too expensive for the rector to maintain and became a private dwelling. One of the new occupiers was Dr. A. J. Cronin, the novelist who is reported to have written *The Citadel* whilst residing at Sullington. Henry retired from the living at the age of ninety-two and died three years later.

*   *   *   *   *

The epitome of the sporting parson was the incumbent of St Margaret's, Rottingdean, who served his parish faithfully for almost half a century. When the visitor enters the church his attention is less likely to be focussed on the altar than on the memorial which stands above the pulpit. It recalls the Rev. Dr. Thomas Redman Hooker, 1762-1838. His was a colourful character and his activities were not confined solely to parochial duties. He was born the son of the owner of the Manor of Tonbridge whose possessions included a slighted castle and a gunpowder mill. Educated at Westminster and Oriel College, Thomas Hooker exhibited an all-round talent as scholar, sportsman and musician and his career prospects appeared dazzling. Unfortunately his expectations were reduced when the gunpowder mills exploded, leaving his father in severely straitened circumstances. He had to concentrate his talents on earning a living.

At first he became private secretary to the Duke of Dorset; then he went to Blois to learn French. After two years away, during which time he conducted two young aristocrats on the Grand Tour of Europe, he returned to England and took Holy Orders, being ordained Deacon in Westminster Abbey in 1784 and Priest in the Temple Church two years later.

The usual curacies followed, and then an opportunity arose. Hooker's former employer, the Duke, who was the patron on many livings, realised that he had two vacancies. Two young clergy in whom he took an interest were seeking preferment and so the Duke suggested that dice should be thrown to decide which should be appointed to each. By this somewhat quixotic arrangement Hooker came to St. Margaret's in 1792 and 'liked its air and situation'.

So began an even more colourful incumbency. His undoubted flair for tutoring was soon put to use, for he enlarged the Vicarage, now The Grange, opposite the village pond, to accommodate pupils and thus augment his stipend. His wife Mary, née Cook, a cousin of Jane Austen, presented him with a son in 1797, but she died soon after. Young John was cared for henceforth by an aunt.

Emma Jane Greenland, Hooker's first cousin, who was a talented artist and a gifted musician, became his second wife in 1801. In 1787 she had been awarded the gold palette of the Society of Arts for her experiments in encaustic painting. Also honoured in the field of music, she had six sonatas for piano and violin dedicated to her by J. C. Bach. The Vicarage must have echoed with chamber music and shone with their colourful works of art.

The school they ran was reputed to have more sons of the nobility than any other. At various times among their pupils were the nephews of the Duke of Wellington and of Napoleon Bonaparte. Others, later to make their mark, included Bulward Lytton, politician and author, and Henry Manning.

As the village was quite small, Hooker's parochial duties were none too arduous and he found time to establish a day school and a Sunday school for local children. However, it was his other extra-pastoral activities that were to give him an even greater reputation. He was undoubtedly involved with the Rottingdean gang of smugglers, acting as an observer of the movements of the revenue men and reporting back with the speed his expert horsemanship would allow.

On one occasion he was drinking in an inn some distance from home and took advantage of bargain-priced bandana kerchiefs offered for sale. The friendly landlord whispered to him that one particular man in the bar was a revenue officer. When Hooker rose to go, the other asked that, as they were to ride in the same direction, if he might accompany him. The Vicar, realising that should the customs man find the smuggled handkerchiefs on him, his horse would be forfeit, thought of a way of escape. During their ride he dropped his riding crop and, pleading advanced age, asked his companion to retrieve it. As soon as the other had dismounted, Hooker was away like the wind, not stopping till he had reached the security of his own stable. A trap-door in the floor of his study allowed undetected access to smugglers' tunnels which lead to his cellars. The reward for his complicity would be a regular supply of smuggled spirits; perhaps Kipling had him in mind when he used the phrase 'Brandy for the Parson' in his poem *A Smuggler's Song*!

Bust of the Rev. Dr. Thomas Redman Hooker.

St. Margaret's, Rottingdean.

So highly was Hooker thought of by the free traders that their leader asked him to take command of the gang in the event of the expected invasion from France. So real was the threat during the Napoleonic wars that the authorities entrusted him with the organising of the evacuation of the local population if the French landed. He arranged for the farm waggons to be used and issued printed tickets assigning individuals to particular carts. One of these, bearing his signature, is displayed at The Grange museum - the former Vicarage.

Hooker's nocturnal activity was no less energetic than his enthusiasm for sport. He was a powerful member of the village cricket team but his greatest enjoyment, almost certainly, was hunting. He was Master of the Brookside Harriers from 1800 to 1820 and his prowess was noted by R. S. Surtees, the chronicler of hunting, who was amazed at Hooker's ability to combine so many diverse activities. He commented on his less-than-conventional hunting attire: 'Instead of the shovel hat, he sported a black velvet cap, and a rifle green coat, with a black sailor's jacket over it, drab smalls, tremendously baggy overalls, and a massive silver jockey-whip'. The fact that he injured his right arm in a hunting accident did not even curtail his musicianship, for he had his cello restrung and learnt to play it with his left hand.

His ministry of forty-six years ended with his death in April 1838. His passing was mourned with a touching poetic tribute in the *Brighton Herald* and his parishioners, whose welfare he always had in mind, contributed to the marble bust and commemorative plaque which is still as dominant a feature in St. Margaret's as he himself was, when pastor.

When the Rev. George Faithful was inducted into the living of Storrington he brought to the parish both spiritual and material benefits for, not only did he prove to be a conscientious pastor, he came accompanied by his army coaching school. Between the years 1868 and 1874 the British Army had been reorganised and, among a variety of reforms, the purchase of commissions had been abolished and entry made subject to examinations. As a result the army class appeared in public schools and 'crammers' establishments for those who needed special tuition.

In consequence, George Faithful arrived in Storrington accompanied by forty-one students, their horses, hounds, grooms and servants. His own household consisted of his wife, six daughters, a governess, a cook, a kitchenmaid, three parlourmaids, three housemaids and a footman. Five of his students lodged with him, the remainder being installed in various houses in the village. There were also five tutors and their households. One of the tutors, the Rev. Frederick Vernon M.A., was described as a clergyman 'without cure of souls but available for Sunday duty'. His house-hold, alone, included his wife, three children, five boarders, a cook, a housemaid, a kitchen-maid and a footman.

The impact of this invasion of a village of about two thousand inhabitants must have been considerable and the cause of some excitement, not least among the unmarried ladies of the neighbourhood! When the 'Faithfullites', as the army students were known, made up a cricket team and played Sullington, the latter scored 93 runs whilst the 'Crammers' reply was 73 for 9, when, presumably, 'bad light stopped play', possibly to the relief of the young gentlemen and to the annoyance of the Sullington rustics.

*   *   *   *   *

One of the outstanding features of the Adur Valley is Lancing College. The story of its foundation as the mother of over fifty associated Woodard Schools is a romance in itself. The story begins with the coming of a curate, Nathaniel Woodard, to St. Mary's parish, Shoreham. Born at Basildon Hall, Essex, and educated at Magdalen Hall, Oxford, he was ordained in 1841. After a curacy in East London, he came to Shoreham in 1847 and the following year founded the St. Nicholas Society. His aim, which became a passion and his life's work, was to establish a series of public schools which would provide a liberal education for the children of the ever-increasing number of middle-class citizens, at fees they could afford.

Nathaniel Woodard has been described as 'neither a very learned person nor a very elegant one'. By nature he was inclined to be stiff and uncompromising. At the same time, he was a man of one idea which he pursued with unflagging energy and sagacity.

Shortly after his arrival in Shoreham, he began a school in the Old Custom House which eventually formed the nucleus of St. John's College, Hurstpierpoint. He also started a school in his own residence prior to the purchase of twenty-three acres of Lancing Hill where, in 1858, the present school was begun. Within the space of twelve years this incredible man had founded three public schools for boys and one for girls. The Woodard Schools have now developed into a network of fifty schools, twelve of which were established during the founder's lifetime.

What was the secret of this extraordinary achievement, surely without parallel in the history of British education?

In addition to unflagging energy and faith in the validity of his ideals, Woodard had a gift of organisation. In some ways he resembled his great predecessor of a hundred years earlier, John Wesley: both had a passion for education; both possessed a genius for organisation; both were driven by a single, consuming passion.

Woodard proved himself to be an extraordinary fund-raiser. Long before the modern methods of fund-raising became almost commonplace, he had conceived the idea of an inaugural luncheon, to be addressed by well-known public figures and accompanied by an appeal for gifts and promises of financial support.

Although it is hard to imagine that the founder ever truly retired, he did come to spend his last years in a large Georgian house in Henfield called Martyn's Lodge.

Across the road, and facing the parish church, stands a thatched cottage whose walls bear rather strange decorations. During Canon Woodard's time it was occupied by an eccentric soldier, Robert Ward, a veteran of the Zulu Wars who, with his brother, kept a cooper's yard not far away. Ward's eccentricities included the practice of sleeping in a bed surrounded by the Ten Commandments and decorating the pear tree in his garden with flags and bunting. He also kept canaries.

It was his belief that Canon Woodard's cat had killed one of his birds and, by way of revenge, he cut out of sheet iron, a series of cats, each with a canary held in its paw. To the metal cats, scallop shells were attached and the whole suspended underneath the eaves on a wire. Whenever the reverend gentleman set off from Martyn's Lodge to go to church, Ward would pull the wire and create an infernal din, hoping, no doubt, to remind Canon Woodard of the feline outrage for which he was held responsible. Not surprisingly, the neighbours complained of the din, but although the practice ceased, the cats remain, now nailed to the walls of this delightful old cottage. Both the cats and the 'Zulu Hole', through which the wire was pulled, are still to be seen.

*   *   *   *   *

One of the minor classics of English literature is surely Kilvert's Diary, the work of the Rev. Francis Kilvert, curate at Clyre, Radnorshire, and Chippenham, Wiltshire, between 1870 and 1879. During these years, he paid at least one visit to West Sussex which he recorded in his diary for 10th and 11th August, 1874.

At the end of that year he recorded how, sitting with his mother 'to see the New Year in', he began to think earnestly of 'dear Katie' and to pray for her. The lady in question, Kate or Kathleen, had been one of five bridesmaids at the wedding in Findon Parish Church of Adelaide Cholmondeley of Worthing; Kilvert, a friend of the bride's brother, had been one of five groomsmen.

At the time, Kilvert, without a living of his own, was acting as his father's curate. He travelled by train from Chippenham to Worthing via Salisbury and, as he journeyed, he admired 'the fair Sussex shore between the sea and the Downs and the gleaners, busy in the golden stubbles, the windmills turning in the sea-breeze'.

Worthing Railway Station, in 1874, won his approval. He found it, 'pretty, light and elegant with its vandyked glass roofs'. On arrival, he drove at once to number eleven, Church Terrace (Gratwicke Road), where it had been arranged for him to stay.

The next day, the bride's brother, Waldo, drove him up the valley to Findon Church where he was advised to wait at the lych-gate for the arrival of the bridesmaids, one of whom was to be 'his companion for the day'. The lady chosen for him proved to be tall and dark with a high aristocratic nose, 'beautiful grey eyes, beautiful white teeth and a sweet, firm, rosy mouth'. She was also blessed with a clear complexion and a face 'something better than handsome'. It would seem to have been a case of 'love at first sight' - though not for the first time in the experience of this somewhat susceptible young clergyman.

After the wedding feast, the whole party drove to Chanctonbury Ring, with Kathleen still Kilvert's 'sweet companion'. Under the lee of the clump he spread his coat on the soft turf and they sat there on the hillside, apart from the rest. Kilvert confessed to have lost his heart 'to the sweetest, noblest, kindest and bravest-hearted girl in England' - something rather remarkable, seeing he had only met her a few hours before!

Kathleen told him she felt that she had known him for a long time; that she loved the works of Tennyson, especially his *In Memoriam*. He felt their souls drawing together on that hillside and prayed that this attraction might ripen into a life-long companionship.

They drove back to Worthing down the steep grass Downs in Kathleen's mother's carriage and, as the wind grew cold and fresh, 'I wrapped my coat round her to keep her warm'. They parted with 'a long, warm clasp of hands'.

The next day dawned clear and beautiful after rain, and Kilvert went for an early walk along the beach. Bathing machines were being run down into the sea; the sailors busy about their boats and nets. He caught the 9:27 morning train out of Worthing with the feeling that he could love God and man better than ever before.

On the Eve of Michaelmas they met again; this time in Bristol. Together they visited the Church of St. Mary, Redcliffe. Alas, the course of their true love was not destined to run smoothly; a poor curate without a living of his own was no suitable match for a pretty young woman of means, and her parents forbade Katie to write to her suitor. What ended their relationship is not clear; suffice to say that, three years after their meeting he was presented to a remote parish in Radnorshire and, in 1877, to that of Bredwardine, Herefordshire. Then in 1879 Kilvert married Elizabeth Anne Rowland of Wotton, near Woodstock, but a month after his wedding he died of peritonitis.

What had happened to Kathleen, and Kilvert's courtship of her, may well have been recorded in two sections of the diary which his wife, Elizabeth, destroyed 'for personal reasons'. Of the twenty-two notebooks he left, only three survive, the rest having been destroyed by a niece of Kilvert's who had inherited them. 'Chanctonbury, sweet Chanctonbury', he had written, 'thou wilt always be a green and beautiful spot in my memory.'

*   *   *   *   *

Two clerics whose names became linked with Brighton were the Rev. Martin Maden and the Rev. F. W. Robertson, who was to become known as 'Robertson of Brighton'.

Maden came from Hertingfordbury Park near Hertford. His mother had been one of John Wesley's early converts and his father, Colonel Maden, once sought a visit from 'Mr. J. Westley' [sic] when he lay seriously ill. Wesley complied and, despite the severity of the weather, journeyed from London to Hertford and ministered 'with truly Christian tenderness'. Their son, who was studying for a legal career, was also converted by Wesley but in a somewhat unorthodox manner.

He was seated with some of his rakish friends in a coffee house when they challenged him to hear John Wesley preach and to produce an impression of him (for young Maden possessed a remarkable gift of mimicry). He took up the challenge but, when his friends asked if he had 'taken the old Methodist off', he had to reply, 'No, but he has taken-off me!' Instead of becoming a lawyer, Martin became ordained, through the influence of a remarkable woman, Selina Hastings, Countess of Huntingdon, also a friend of the Wesley brothers. In their company he associated with other Anglican clergymen who had joined with Wesley in his crusade- men like Henry Venn, William Romaine, and George Whitefield. Maden came to be known as one of the most celebrated of those young men who came under the Countess of Huntingdon's patronage.

The Countess of Huntingdon was certainly a remarkable character in a century which produced so many remarkable people. The Rev. John Fletcher of Madeley - a most saintly man who might have become Wesley's successor, described her, somewhat ironically, as 'a modern prodigy, a pious and humble countess'. In the eyes of Robert Walpole, the eighteenth-century statesman, she seemed to be like 'an old basket-woman who had trampled on her coronet' but she never lost that air of authority which was characteristic of persons of high birth in the eighteenth century. At the same time she was convinced that God had called her to be a missionary to the members of her social class. She began to hold meetings of a religious character which the wits called spiritual 'routs' or 'fashionable assemblies'. In 1749 Robert Walpole's son, Horace, observed that 'Methodism in the Metropolis is more fashionable than anything but Brag', adding that 'the women play very deep at both'. These spiritual routs took place in the drawing rooms of elegant people rather like the Oxford Group meetings of the 1930's. When they reduced theatre revenues, the thespian reaction was to brand George Whitefield as 'a lewd and canting hypocrite'.

The particular brand of Methodism which came to attract Selina was the Calvinistic one, so strongly assailed by John Wesley. But to those of her own class, who wished to retain the privileges of rank and class and at the same time enjoy the comforts of religion, this must have had special appeal. Did not Calvinism teach that one's station in life was the outcome of an Eternal Decree and therefore not to be regretted nor apologised for? John Wesley's Arminianism, with its proclamation that the aristocracy had hearts as sinful 'as the common wretches that crawl on the Earth' (or so the Duchess of Buckingham complained to Selina), 'and that God's offer of salvation through Christ was for one and all, irrespective of social rank, was highly offensive and insulting'. Or so the Duchess wrote in reply to an invitation to attend one of the Countess's drawing-room meetings.

In extension of her work, the Countess of Huntingdon built three chapels, including one at Brighton. (In order to build it, the Countess sold some of her jewels.) It was in this chapel that the Rev. Martin Maden was called to minister. Not only was he rich, he was gifted with a remarkable eloquence and, like another of Selina's young men, George Whitefield, Martin was also the possessor of a fine voice, a splendid presence and excellent manners. He had musical gifts, and a passion for Handel. All these qualities would commend him to a fashionable congregation. So far as his preaching was concerned, John Wesley once heard him and voted his sermon as excellent. He even described him as one who 'both preaches and lives the gospel'.

It may be that John had reason to revise his opinion for, in that period of Methodist history when the Wesleys' preaching was marked by what some could describe as hysterical responses, Maden was rather sceptical about it all. He wondered whether these outpourings were of God or of the devil. And when Maden produced and published a book entitled *A Defence of Polygamy*, it must have made more than a dent in their relationship, however acceptable it may have proved to the Prince of Wales. Maden's patroness, the Countess, implored him to withdraw it from publication and quoted three thousand names of persons who were opposed to it. Maden replied that were there six thousand protestors, the publication would proceed. It is interesting to note that, more than twenty years on, John Wesley noted in his diary that he had 'read Maden' - one wonders which of his works!

The Countess had built her original chapel next door to the house she had taken in North Street, Brighton, on account of the illness of her fourth son. She arranged for other distinguished clergy to preach there and such was their appeal that, within six years, the chapel had to be enlarged. During these years, those who attended her spiritual routs included the Prince of Wales, the Duke of Cumberland and the Lords North, Chatham, Chesterfield and Bolingbroke, plus the Duchess of Marlborough and Lady Suffolk. It was said that the Countess 'interested the curious and claimed the serious'. Among her converts was the Earl of Dartmouth, President of the Royal Society.

One of her preachers was Rev. John Berridge, senior fellow of Clare College, Cambridge, and a noted wit who used his humour to enliven his sermons. On one occasion he even dared to suggest that John Wesley and George Whitefield continued to pursue an itinerant ministry because 'The Lord in his mercy sent them a brace of ferrets', meaning that, unlike Charles Wesley, they were uncomfortably married.

In a day when the aristocracy were held in awe by the lower orders, John Wesley and his friends were not over-impressed by rank and lineage. Indeed, on at least one occasion John noted in his journal that, having observed members of the upper classes in his congregation, he endeavoured to reduce the level of his discourse to that of their understanding. It may well be that it was his disdain for aristocratic privilege as well as antipathy to Lady Huntingdon's Calvinism which kept him away from Brighton. (In fact he used to refer to Calvin's Institutes as 'the horrible decrees'.)

Other ministers in charge of the Brighton chapel were the Rev. J. Sortain, from 1838-1860, and following him, Rev. J. B. Figgis, from 1861 until not long before he died in 1916. It had been rebuilt in 1870, the Earl of Shaftesbury laying the foundation stone, and although this beautiful chapel was demolished in 1972 there are still a number of chapels in the county which originated in connection with the Countess of Huntingdon.

The Countess died in 1791 but Brighton was to find another distinguished preacher in the Rev. F. W. Robertson, who came to be known as 'Robertson of Brighton'. He ministered in a small proprietary chapel known as Trinity and his influence spread far and wide. In a sense he was a pioneer of the Christian Socialist school of thought. But the year 1848 was unpropitious for that particular emphasis. It was the year of revolutions, an age of widespread social turmoil in France, in Italy, in Austria, in Saxony and in England with the rise of the Chartist movement. His lectures on social subjects provoked much opposition, believed by some to have led to his early death at the age of thirty-seven. But during his Brighton ministry he found much comfort in the power of the Sussex countryside 'to calm, if not to purify, the hearts of those who lived there'.

* * * * *

In the annals of church building there can hardly have been two more more remarkable men than the Rev. Henry Wagner and his son Arthur. Henry came from a line of wealthy hatters who served royalty and aristocracy in Europe and in England. His father, Melchior, hatter to George III, had married the daughter of Henry Mitchell, the Vicar of Brighton. Their son Henry was born in 1792 and after tutoring the sons of the Duke of Wellington, he also became Vicar of Brighton, taking up his living in 1824. His ministry was remarkable for his strongly held Tory views in a predominantly Whig environment, and for his determination to provide 'free' pews in his churches for the rapidly growing number of poor parishioners. He recognised that normal pew rents were a luxury many townsfolk could not afford.

His wealth allowed him to build six churches, the most notable of which, and one of the only two surving, was St. Paul's in West Street. Costing £14,000, it was built between 1846 and 1848 in Gothic style, in contrast to the popular classic form fashionable in Georgian time, and was intended for his son, Arthur, ordained in 1849. Initially it was a bare shell but when Arthur was promoted from 'Perpetual Curate' to Vicar in 1873, he set about its transformation to a place suitable for the high church rituals which he favoured. Kempe and Pugin designed the stained glass, Carpenter and Bodley, the interiors and Edward Burne-Jones the triptych.

The rituals associated with such an ornate church aroused passionate opposition in the community. Arthur also stirred controversy when, at the trial of Constance Kent for the murder of her half-brother, he refused to divulge what she had disclosed in the confessional. He was assaulted in the street and even shot at.

Arthur added five more churches to the six which his father had built but he also used his wealth for housing developments to improve the lot of the less fortunate. His most remarkable project was the construction, in brick, of St. Bartholomew's, which has the tallest nave in the country and creates an impression of immense size and strange beauty. It was not without its critics, however, being dubbed 'Wagner's Folly' and 'Noah's Ark'. Undeterred he embarked on St. Martin's in Lewes Road, in memory of his father, who had died in 1870.

Although many of the churches created by father and son have been demolished, the impact which they had on the religous life of the town for so long was truly immense. Arthur died in 1902, a figure of controversy during his life, but one honoured for the selflessness shown by his great generosity to the underprivileged. He and his father have lasting memorials in their remaining churches in Brighton, a town which owes much to them.

*　*　*　*　*

The Baptists were, and still are, strong in the county. One of the more extraordinary of this fraternity was John Burgess, glove- and breeches-maker and a Particular Baptist preacher. He lived in Ditchling and, whilst undoubtedly a keen Christian, did not exclude worldly pursuits from his interests. He kept a diary in which he described a cricket match on Lindfield Common where, on 1st August 1785, Lindfield played Sussex County. A few years later he recounted going to a 'bull-bait' at Fryeroake [sic] where his dog was accounted the best of five or six 'and received no hurt'. This appears to have been followed by a good dinner consisting of 'A round of Beef Boiled a good piece roasted and a hag of mutten & Ham of Pork & plum pudden plenty of wine & punch'. Afterwards he went to Brighton and had a wash in the sea.

Ditchling had long been a stronghold of dissent. A chapel was built in 1740 and a free school established in 1815. At a love-feast in 1753, one of the preachers was John Burgess In 1788 he had not lost his love for life and enjoyed another visit to Brighton. It was the Duke of York's birthday and, as well as cricket, there was stoolball, football, dancing, fireworks, two roasted oxen, bread and beef, and strong beer. In the previous year he had described meeting for three or four hours with friends, 'in moral and religious conversation' regarding the Christian evidences - the existence and attributes of the Supreme Being - and agreeing that they should meet for a like purpose every Monday between the hours of four and eight. John Burgess was plainly a man of many parts. His chapel and its burial ground are still to be found in Ditchling, 'up a twitten from East End Lane'.

Cats House, Henfield.

John Selden's birthplace as portrayed about 1840.

IX   STATESMEN, POLITICIANS AND REFORMERS

The list of Sussex folk, whether native-born or immigrant, who have held high offices of State is truly formidable. It includes Prime Ministers, Chancellors of the Exchequer, First Lords of the Admiralty and Post-Masters General.

Sir John Gage was a trusted friend of Henry VIII and his family and, as Constable of the Tower of London, had been the custodian of the tragic Lady Jane Grey and also of the young Elizabeth. His portrait and the family memorials are to be seen in West Firle Church and in the family home in Firle Park.

Henry Bowyer of Cuckfield Place had been Controller of Henry VIII's household.

During the reign of the first Elizabeth there was a lawyer, Thomas Byshopp, a native of Henfield, who first rented, and finally bought, Parham Park from the Palmer family. At one time he had been secretary to Frances Walsingham, the Queen's chief 'spy-catcher', who, through his spies, had discovered the Babington Plot, a discovery which led to the execution of the Queen of Scots.

From Buckhurst Park, Withyham, came Thomas Sackville, Lord Treasurer to the often parsimonious Elizabeth I.

During the Stuart period, Charles Sergison of Cuckfield Park succeeded Samuel Pepys as Commissioner and Clerk to the Acts of the Navy whilst, after the Restoration of Charles II, Henry Byshopp, son of Thomas, was made Post-Master General. Although he held the post for only three years, he made his mark in the form of the first postmark indicating the day and the month of a letter's posting. The idea was to prevent the 'letter-carryers' (as they were known) from retaining letters from post to post.

Lloyd George was associated with one of the most beautiful and most interesting of the great houses of Sussex - Danny, near Hurstpierpoint. It was built towards the end of the Elizabethan Age and unlike Parham and Wiston, built of red brick rather than stone. The name Danny is said to originate in Danegthe, or Swinepasture, and after George Goring of Eades had built it, the house passed into the possession of the Courthopes. Subsequently, the Campion family owned it for many years.

In 1918 Danny had been let to Lord Riddell who lent it to Lloyd George, and there are still those who remember him walking in Hurstpierpoint. On a November day in 1918 the War Cabinet, which included Winston Churchill, Bonar-Law, A. J. Balfour, Lord Milner, Admiral Wemyss and Sir Henry Wilson, met in the Prime Minister's room (the Prime Minister being in bed with a cold), and cabled President Wilson the terms of the Armistice, advising him to proceed with negotiations. At the same time Sir William Campion was preparing his brigade for a fresh attack to be launched on 12th November, ignorant of the fact that in his old home decisions had been made which would save the lives of many of the troops he commanded.

Robert Banks Jenkinson, second Earl of Liverpool, held the post of Prime Minister for fifteen stormy years. During his time of office his ministry was marred by the Massacre of Peterloo, the trial of Queen Caroline, wife of George IV, and the Cato Street Conspiracy which aimed at the assassination of the Cabinet.

Lord Liverpool bought Buxted Park during his years of office and, not liking the near-presence of the village of Buxted, had it removed outside the boundaries of his property and away from the parish church.

Another Sussex landowner, George Joachim Goschen, who had an estate near Flimwell, East Sussex, became Chancellor of the Exchequer. He was the son of a Jewish merchant of German extraction.

During Lord Salisbury's administration, Goschen was invited to succeed Lord Randolph Churchill in that office but, when offered the purchase of the former Chancellor's robe, he declined. Lord Randolph was reported to have said that this was the first time he had known a Jew refuse to do a deal in old clothes. Goschen had his own robe made and many years later, in 1981, all its fifteen-pounds' weight of silk and gold was worn by Sir Geoffrey Howe in his capacity of Master of the Mint.

* * * * *

One of the saddest stories regarding officers of the State who have lived in Sussex, relates to Sidney Charles Buxton, first Earl of Newtimber and, through the tragic deaths of both his sons, the last.

'It hardly seems possible', wrote Barbara Willard in her book about Sussex, 'that one generation could have endured so much sorrow'. The tragic story can be read in memorials found in the early English Church of St. John across the road from Newtimber Place. It tells how one son died whilst leading his company in Flanders during the Great War; the other son, a great lover of nature, died while young of peritonitis. Their only sister died in childbirth.

Earl Buxton, a Liberal M.P., had been President of the Board of Trade, Post-Master General and also Governor-General of South Africa. He came from a great nineteenth-century political family, being the grandson of Fowell Buxton, one of the abolitionists associated with William Wilberforce. Fowell Buxton also chaired the first meeting of the Royal Society for the Prevention of Cruelty to

Animals, whose aims were the protection of defenceless creatures against ill-treatment by human beings.

In the year 1955, a very old thatched cottage in Salvington, Worthing, was first gutted by fire and then demolished by order of the authorities. Had it been preserved, it could well have become a shrine for, in the year 1584, it was the birthplace of John Selden, later to achieve fame as an historian, a jurist and a wit.

The son of a farmer of Lacies Farm, he must have been a precocious lad for, by the age of fourteen years, he was admitted to Hart Hall, in the University of Oxford. When about nineteen he was admitted a member of Clifford's Inn and later the Inner Temple.

His first publication was a history of England with the title *Analecton Anglo-Britannicon*; this won him an immediate reputation as an up-and-coming young man. In the field of literature, he annotated Michael Drayton's *Poly-Olbion*, a great topographical poem in the course of which the poet pleaded for the conservation of the Wealden forests.

But it was in the field of law and politics that Selden was to make his mark. He became a Member of Parliament and was appointed to prepare articles of impeachment against George Villiers, Duke of Buckingham. That was in 1626 and, in 1643, the Long Parliament made him an assessor at the synod appointed to reform the English Church, known as the Westminster Assembly of Divines. Selden used to say that he went to Westminster in order to observe the ancient Persian sport - 'wild asses fighting'. He was the author of the *History of Tythes* which indicated that the parson's revenue derived from tythes had no justification in law. Naturally, this raised a storm of protest.

But his greatest triumph came at the end of a long struggle, which he and Edward Coke had begun, in the endeavour to subject the legality of the King's actions to the judgment of those courts which administered the Common Laws. It was a victory for civilisation; a defeat for the irresponsible use of power.

Far from being a dour Puritan, Selden was almost as famous as Samuel Johnson for his *Table Talk*. He was wont to compare old friends to old shoes observing that 'they were easiest on the feet... And therefore best'. Regarding the accepted mode of kissing a lady's hand, he said: 'Methinks to kiss their hands after their lips, as some do, is like little boys who, after they eat the apple, fall to the paring'. As regards religion, he was tolerant in an age of intolerance. 'Religion', he said 'is like fashion: One man wears his doublet slashed, another laced, another plain; but every man has a doublet. We differ about the trimming'.

It was the opinion of Hugo de Groot, a distinguished lawyer who was a member of the Dutch Embassy in London, that Selden was 'a great man and the friend of great men; the best endowed with common sense of any writer'. He was not opposed to the monarchy as an institution but believed it should be a constitutional one.

Although Selden's name is well known in Worthing and appears in Selden Lane, Selden's Way, the Selden Arms in Lyndhurst Road, the John Selden in Durrington, Selden Road and the John Selden Schools at Goring, it rather seems that this distinguished jurist and maker of history was, like the proverbial prophet, unrecognised by his own people.

* * * * *

Another Sussex lad, born, like Selden, into a farming family and destined to become an even more famous figure in the life of the nation, was Richard Cobden. An outstanding feature of his life was that his accomplishments, unlike those of Selden, were achieved without the advantages of a higher education.

He was born at Dunford Farm, near Heyshott, Sussex, the fourth of eleven children. Perhaps it was on this account that he was sent to live with an uncle at Barnard Castle, Yorkshire. It was during the days when Charles Dickens was moved to expose the conditions in some of the Yorkshire schools with his tale of Dotheboys Hall and Mr. Wackford Squeers. Certainly, young Cobden endured five years of being ill-fed, ill-treated and ill-educated. It was whilst Dickens stayed at the King's Head in Barnard Castle that he forged his great indictment of similar conditions.

One of the effects of this experience, so far as Cobden was concerned, was to endow him with a passionate concern for the improvement of opportunities of education for all, thus pioneering the 1870 Education Act.

On leaving school, he served for some years as the representative of a London-based commercial house. But it was not long before he had launched out on his own account. He built, some thirty miles north of Manchester in the village of Slabden, a calico-printing works.

Cobden was then elected to Parliament and made his maiden speech in 1841, by which time he had become the most travelled member of the Commons. It was through his advocacy that the repeal of the Corn Laws was brought about and it is for this, he is chiefly remembered. The laws, which imposed a duty on the importation of corn, fell most heavily on the poorest. Cobden had already become a leading member of the Anti-Corn Law League and this was the subject of his maiden speech. When, about five years later, the laws were repealed, Cobden was hailed as the champion of the poor.

All his political activity had left little time for supervision of his own business with the result that he found it on the verge of bankruptcy. Financial ruin was averted when a grateful nation came to the rescue with a subscription of eighty thousand pounds, a gigantic sum in those days. Part of the money was used to rebuild his old home, Dunford Farm, in its present form. It is now beautifully preserved as a conference centre under the control of the Y.M.C.A.

According to Gladstone's biographer, John Morley, Cobden ranked with Disraeli and Gladstone as a man of outstanding ability and the source of original views; he also credited him with 'the most persuasive tongue in Europe'. Cobden was remembered as a man of quiet disposition, modest, genial, and one who avoided the life of high society, even refusing to wear court dress. He was a lover of Sussex and found nothing in nature so beautiful as the wooded parts of his native county. In the Heyshott Parish Church of St. James may be seen a memorial and a metal plaque indicating Cobden's habitual seat in the church. He is described as a great English-man and a pioneer of international understanding and peace.

* * * * *

It was two young women from Sussex who formed part of the advance guard of the feminist movement whose patron saint must surely have been Mary Wollstonecraft, Mary Shelley's mother, who, in 1791, had produced her *Vindication of the Rights of Women*, a book which, at the time, created a furore and was banned from the homes of respectable families. The names of the Sussex young ladies were Sarah Emily Davies and Barbara Bodichon, née Leigh-Smith.

They were born into a male-dominated society, a situation which was widely accepted even by women. For instance, Charlotte Yonge, a popular lady novelist, with a hundred titles to her name, once said that she had no hesitation in declaring her 'full belief in the inferiority of women'. The Queen had declared that the subject of women's rights made her so furious she could scarcely contain herself. The fact was that a married woman, in those days, was a 'legal nonentity': she possessed no property and was not allowed to sign a contract or a will without her husband's accompanying signature. It was generally believed that God and nature had submerged her existence in that of her husband's - an idea which Emily Davies, Barbara Bodichon, Elizabeth Garrett (Anderson) and others refused to admit.

Sarah Emily Davies was the daughter of a distinguished scholar and clergyman, the Rev. Dr. John Davies. At one time he had been curate of St. Pancras and St. John, Chichester, and subsequently at East Ashling but, being a Low Churchman, had fallen foul of the Archdeacon, H. E. Manning (later Cardinal Manning).

His daughter, Emily, was a dainty little lady, demure yet firm. In later years she became known among her students as 'the despot of decorum' - when the girls wished to perform the plays of

Shakespeare with those playing male parts proposing to appear in tights, Miss Davies put her foot down.

But her ruling passion was that university education, such as had been enjoyed both by her father and by her two brothers, should be available to women. In her youth there were but four universities in England, none of which accepted women.

After having nursed her sister Jane, until she died, Emily immediately set off to nurse one of her brothers in Algiers, where she met Barbara Bodichon whose father, Benjamin Leigh-Smith, M.P. for Norwich, owned a house there. The two ladies found that their views on the subjection of their sex coincided and, at Barbara's London home in Blandford Square, Emily was introduced to Bessie Parkes (destined to become the mother of Hilaire Belloc) and a newly-formed society for the promotion of the employment of women.

Barbara's father had long held advanced views on the rights of women (even though he denied that of matrimony to the mother of his large family!). When he died, Barbara found herself a wealthy woman and subsequently used some of her money to build a cottage on the family estate in Sussex, known as Scalands. This was used as a holiday home for the workers of women's rights. (See Chapter VI.)

Believing that a big step towards their ideal would be to secure higher education for women, they bought Benslow House, Hitchin, and established a women's college, two of the teachers or tutors being Emily Davies and George Eliot. Visiting professors included Dr. Hort and Professor Seeley from the University of Cambridge. In 1873 the college moved from Hitchin to the parish of Girton, two or three miles from the centre of Cambridge. There they commenced the building of Girton College, into which Barbara poured thousands of pounds of her wealth and of which Emily was made first Mistress. Her photograph, attired in an academic gown and topped with a white bonnet, is to be seen in the college today.

It took several years before the university could be persuaded to allow Girton girls to take its examinations and sixty years elapsed before Girton was admitted as a college of the University. Emily lived to see this, though Barbara did not. She did, however, have the satisfaction of seeing the Married Women's Property Act give equal rights to spinsters and widows. The admission of Girton was brought about, in part, by the pressure of public opinion and partly by the demonstration by its students of their ability to compete with men academically. Their elation at some of the earlier successes led them to ring the college bells so energetically that they brought out the fire-brigade!

Brickwall House, Northiam.
Reproduced by kind permission of Mrs. M. Parsons.

X   THE PASSING CENTURIES

In its strict sense a cavalcade is a procession of horsemen, but in this book we have adopted the more general meaning of a series of people and events passing in review for us to admire. Not that everything that happened in Sussex was admirable, but whatever the moving sequence of history, every part of the succession contributed to the legacy of the county which we have inherited.

Sussex can justly claim to have almost the longest history of any part of Britain, for soon after the ice began to retreat at the end of the (Pleistocene) Ice Age, groups of nomadic peoples moved in. However, long before that, there is proof positive that early man, *Homo erectus*, flaked flint tools at Boxgrove, near Chichester, to help his chances of survival. From an interglacial, a period of comparative warmth, evidence has been unearthed of the butchery of animals such as rhinoceros some 450,000 years ago.

With the last and, possibly, final retreat of the ice sheets, about 10,000 years ago, our landscape began to respond to a more sustained effort by a few wandering groups to subsist on berries and other fruit, roots and small game. At that time what is now Southern Britain, was still joined to the Continent by a land bridge and north-western migration from Europe was easy. Rising sea-levels, triggered by ice-melt, then isolated us from the main land mass and newcomers would have had to cross an ever-widening channel.

However, Neolithic (New Stone Age) peoples came in increasing numbers and were the first to leave clear marks of their life and work on the impressionable Downs. Mineshafts were driven down to reach the flint layers of the best quality for the knapping of sickle blades, arrow and harpoon heads and scrapers. Causewayed camps appeared on the skyline as did the long barrows - burial mounds - in which local chieftains 'overlook' their territories throughout eternity. Their efforts, as with those of the later Bronze Age and Iron Age tribes can still be deciphered on the landscape; the clearance of the woodland which had slowly colonised the chalklands as the ice retreated had begun in earnest.

The Long Man of Wilmington.

Tribal society in the Iron Age was highly organised: defensive forts of revetted earth embankments were thrown up, and well-defined areas of authority became established. These were the tribes which

119

held the land when the Romans came. The expeditions of Julius Caesar in 55 and 54 B.C. did not touch what is now Sussex, and it was not until almost a century later that the invasion inspired by the Emperor Claudius, in A.D.43, that one of the spearheads of the conquering legions came to change life dramatically.

One of the local tribe chieftains, Cogidubnus, realising that he could not match the might of Roman arms, became an ally, and the area prospered. Initially the galleys came up the creeks to the west of the Manhood peninsula of Selsey and set up an army base at Fishbourne, from which the subjugation of the south-west was begun. Vespasian, the commander, (and later an emperor), built a villa near Bosham. Not long after the area was firmly secured, a great complex was established at Fishbourne to honour the man who by then had been accorded the title of Claudius Tiberius Cogidubnus. The Mediterranean-style building set in the coastal plain grew to palatial proportions; the community prospered for some two centuries.

The Barbican Gate.

Owing to the rising sea levels, however, this tribal capital on Selsey Bill was destroyed by marine erosion, so the Roman built for his people a new town, *Noviomagus* Reg(i)norum ('the new town of the Regni') nearby. Chichester, as it was later called, was thus established as the first truly urban site in Sussex. It possessed all the amenities of civilised life - public buildings, temples, baths, luxurious villas and, just outside the walls, an ampitheatre in which the games were presented for expatriate Romans and the local population. A road network was developed, and Stane Street, joining *Noviomagus* with *Londinium*, was built in A.D. 71. Along its length, at intervals, were posting stations which allowed those on imperial business to rest and relax overnight.

Other new roads radiated from the Thames valley, and a cross way, the Greensand route, followed the foot of the escarpment of the Downs. Villas proliferated as peace brought plenty, both in food - corn, meat and milk, and in the iron goods of the Inner Weald. Luxuries were imported from the Empire to beautify houses and gardens of the patricians. The villa at Bignor was surely one of the finest, with lovely mosaics, fountains and ornamental gardens in the centre of productive and varied farmland. Perhaps the gladiators represented on a mosaic in the Venus room expressed the owner's support for the combat in the ampitheatre at *Noviomagus*.

Towards the end of the third century, life became less secure with the onset of predatory raids by Saxons from the Rhineland. To counteract the very real threat of invasion, the Romans set up a defence system on the Channel coasts in which a series of forts were built. These 'forts of the Saxon Shore' were established from East Anglia to Hampshire, and one, Anderita, 'the great ford', was built on an oval promontory which projected into the then haven of Pevensey. The whole enterprise was under the control of Carausius, a man who had risen through the ranks because of his skills both as soldier and sailor. His task was to intercept Saxon raiders, but he saw an opportunity for great personal gain by leaving the interception until after the raids, whereupon he relieved the Saxons of their booty. He was arraigned on charge of treason by his old master, the Emperor Maximian, but such was his power - and his popularity with his men - that he was able declare himself Emperor of the western part of the empire.

At that time the sea lapped against the low cliff below the defensive walls of the fort, which, later, in about A.D. 340, were strengthened with stone and flint. The outer wall is still in an exceptionally sound state of repair. By A.D. 410 the Romans were no longer able to afford the expense of maintaining an army to protect Britain, and so civilised life slowly began to crumble, leaving the area open to invasion and settlement by Saxon peoples.

They arrived, according to the Anglo-Saxon Chronicles, in A.D. 477, when Aelle and his sons, Cissa, Wlenc and Cymen, landed with their followers on the Selsey peninsula. After determined and fierce campaigning, Aelle established supreme authority over much of the south, and his people began the settlement which moved gradually from the coastal lands into the Weald. These were the lands of the 'sud-Seaxe' - transposed later to 'Sussex'. The colonisation sequence of the county can be traced by the place names which they bestowed, and which, in gradually altered form, we have inherited. The Saxons themselves took their own name from the 'seaxe', a greatly favoured multi-purpose long knife or short sword.

Initially pagan, the Saxons were grudgingly converted to Christianity by the efforts of such monks as Dicul and his brethren who set up a church at Bosham about A.D. 660, and a little later by the efforts of Wilfrid, a northern bishop, who came as a missionary to convert the heathen. A perverse pride made the Saxons boast that they were among the last to be turned to the ways of the Lord. A simple life, in rough timber and thatch huts, was the norm for many centuries although later on, increasing prosperity allowed the building of more substantial churches in local stone and flint.

The vicissitudes of national life were reflected in the local scene. Canute, a Scandinavian monarch, certainly owned a property in Bosham and probably improved the church there. Subsequently his liegeman, Earl Godwin, inherited the mansion which was passed down to his son, Harold Godwinson. The waterside two-storey house is shown in the Bayeux Tapestry in the scene before and after Harold's journey to Normandy in 1064, during which Duke William extracted Harold's alleged promise of fealty.

What followed altered the course of English history, and much of the action was focused on Sussex. William's invasion made landfall at Pevensey, where the Roman walls of Anderita provided the unopposed force with a secure hold until the army moved on to Hastings, where a simple motte and keep was thrown up in days. Harold was extraordinarily unlucky in that he was fighting off a Scandinavian invasion in Yorkshire when news of William's arrival reached him. He marched the remains of his army back south as speedily as he had moved north and intercepted William's progress in a day-long engagement on 14th October, 1066 at the place later named Battle. It could have gone either way. Eventually, at dusk, the Normans and their allies triumphed and an alien yoke was placed on the shoulders of resentful Anglo-Saxons.

Anderita Gateway.

The whole series of events is depicted with vigour and style in the Bayeux Tapestry. This embroidery, the stitchwork of which was almost certainly created by nuns in Canterbury, was commissioned by the Conqueror's half-brother, Bishop Odo. He displayed it in his cathedral at Bayeux, where it remained on view for a few weeks annually - a tradition held for many centuries. The tapestry carrying the echoes of early medieval valour down through the ages, owes its miraculous survival to the fact that it was rolled up for storage in between airings. It is now displayed in the William the Conqueror Centre in Bayeux. An almost exact replica, the Leek Tapestry, created in the 1880's, may be viewed at Reading Museum.

William decreed that a magnificent abbey should be built on the ridge so valiantly defended by Harold, with its high altar at the very spot at which Harold had been slain. The Abbey at Battle became a place of pilgrimage and it survived until the dissolution of the monasteries. The walls, which earlier had proudly held the roll of honour of Norman knights, were destroyed after Henry VIII gave the sacred buildings to Sir Anthony Browne. He turned the monks out of their cloisters; the last brother to leave invoked a curse by which Browne's family was to be ended by fire and water.

The shadow of the curse became reality more than two centuries later: Cowdray House, Midhurst, once owned by Sir Anthony - the first Viscount Montagu - burned down in 1793, destroying Battle Abbey's Roll of Honour, which had been saved and held at Cowdray; a week after, Viscount Montagu drowned in the Rhine. His sister inherited the ruin of Cowdray House and her two sons perished in the sea at Bognor. Coincidence or something more sinister?

Norman rule was imposed on Sussex, by a series of administrative units called rapes, which ran north to south across the county. Each was controlled from a castle by one of the new king's trusted barons, and each castle was given a defensive outer ring of smaller motte and bailey structures. Chichester's stronghold had disappeared, but the remainder, at Arundel, Bramber, Lewes, Pevensey and Hastings, may be seen in varying degrees of survival.

At Lewes, which, unusually, had two mottes and two keeps, William de Warenne and his wife, Gundrada, wished to give thanks for the success of the papally-supported crusade against Harold. They travelled as pilgrims, without the trappings of rank and wealth, towards Rome. Local wars prevented them from reaching their intended destination. They diverted to Cluny, in Burgundy, where they were greatly impressed by the Benedictine abbey. Eventually they obtained permission to create a daughter house beneath their castle at Lewes, with the result that a magnificent Cluniac Priory, dedicated to St. Pancras, the patron of an earlier church on the site, arose on the edge of the meadows of the River Ouse at Southover. It was one of the most glorious expressions of ecclesiastical architecture in the whole of England.

The group of buildings standing isolated from the walled town above must have been awe-inspiring to the simple peasantry. The flint and clunch cores of the walls were clad first in stone brought from the Isle of Wight and then with cream Caen stone brought from Normandy, up the Ouse and along the little Cockshut stream. Besides the great monastic church, the nave of which was longer than that of Chichester Cathedral today, there were grouped the Chapter House, a wonderful cloister, a hospitium by the gate, a refectory, the dorter - a dormitory for the brothers - and the rere-dorter for their ablutions, as well as a lodging for the Prior where he could entertain important guests in the style to which they were accustomed. From the priory the black-robed brothers would be able to go out into the Sussex countryside to visit village churches, some of which they undoubtedly helped to decorate.

This great centre of religious life was but one of many which burgeoned in the years following the conquest. In addition to the Benedictines there were Cistercians, Dominicans, Franciscans and Carmelites all following their own particular observances in houses from Durford to Rye and from Bayham to Arundel. Whilst most were the domain of men, three were nunneries under the guidance of an Abbess or a Prioress. The monasteries grew fabulously wealthy and later some of the monks enjoyed a much higher standard of living than their vows should have permitted.

The Priory of St. Pancras had a part to play in another significant episode of English history. King Henry III had, in the eyes of some of the nobility, reneged upon an agreement. Simon de Monfort resolved to confront the King and intercepted him at Lewes where, on 14th May 1264, a battle was fought. Before this the king rested at the priory whilst his son, Prince Edward, remained in the castle above. Early in the morning Edward was alerted to one of the enemy columns cresting Offham hill. He immediately went out, sending word to his father before chasing the London contingent back down into the Weald.

This proved to be a critical error of judgement, for by the time Henry III had reached the Downs, he was confronted by further columns led by de Monfort. Without Edward's support the royal army crumbled, being forced to retreat to the Priory, where the Mise of Lewes was signed - by which the Parliament of 1265 was convened at Westminster. Of about twenty thousand troops who fought, almost a quarter perished. Many of the injured were nursed at the Priory and many who did not were buried in a pit where they remained until in 1846, excavations through the Priory grounds for the Brighton to Lewes railway exposed the grisly reminder.

The whole story is retold by Tufton Beamish in *Battle Royal* published by Frederick Muller in 1965. Sir Tufton, later Lord Chelwood, Member for Lewes, gave a striking memorial to the town in the form of a Norman helmet, intersected by a cross, around the top of which scenes from the battle are depicted in bas-relief. It may be seen in the Priory grounds. Sadly, like all similar monasteries, the Cluniac Priory was destroyed by Henry VIII's chancellor, Thomas Cromwell, in 1538, and the few pathetic walls which remained are now being carefully restored and preserved by the Lewes Priory Trust.

The Norman occupation had a further consequence for Sussex for, in common with most English counties, it was assessed in the Domesday Book, our earliest public record, which was published in 1086. The task of the commissioners who travelled the countryside was to take evidence, on oath, to record a full survey of land-holding. An authoritative register of possessions and land use, it is thus an invaluable document which sheds light on an economy more than 900 years old.

The Domesday Book is a delight to amateur historians and geographers as well as a source book for the professional. The Sussex volume, with the rest of the counties, was reproduced under the editorship of John Morris, by the Chichester publishers, Phillimore, in 1976.

The long centuries after the Norman conquest saw the slow transformation of a landscape from one shaped by a predominantly farming economy, through an industrial era to the much diversified life of modern Sussex. This began with the opening up of the county to outside influences first by turnpike and canal, then by rail and a rejuvenation of the road system.

The first great impact on the inner landscape was the modernisation of an ancient industry - iron working. The low-grade clay ironstone and ferruginous 'pans' had been worked ever since the pre-historic Iron Age. Roman bloomeries provided material for export along the road to London and to a port in the Newhaven-Seaford area. The industry was revitalised with the introduction of new blast furnace techniques in the last decade of the XVth century.

The Wealden landscape was devastated by the felling of great trees for the making of charcoal used in the smelting process. A view from the downland scarp would have revealed smoke from the charcoal burners camps and the occasional flash of flame as a furnace was opened. A sharp-eared observer might also have heard the rhythmic clang of the enormous hammers. Iron masters thrived and many beautiful houses made from Wealden sandstone were raised as a testament to their increasing wealth.

The prized iron goods they manufactured included horseshoes and nails, wheel-rims and cauldrons, cannon and shot, firebacks and grave-slabs. Indeed it was in Sussex that the first cast-iron cannon was made in 1543. Previously cannons had been made of iron strips bound with bands and these had a disturbing tendency to disintegrate explosively. The new technique revolutionised the efficiency of ordnance.

Another family which grew wealthy from iron, in the early years was that of the great character 'Mad Jack' Fuller whose eccentricities produced the so-called 'follies' two hundred years later. These are dotted around his estate near Brightling. Such was his patronage of the church there that he was allowed to build, long before his death, a pyramid tomb twenty-five feet high in Brightling churchyard. When eventually he died it was rumoured that he was buried in frock-coat and top-hat, sitting at a table on which was a decanter. Sadly, later investigation showed this to be a fiction.

Yet another ironmaster was Richard Woodman who, because of his Protestant belief was martyred at the stake in Lewes during the Marian persecution of Protestants in 1557.

Fears that over-use of the Wealden woodland would jeopardise England's shipbuilding led to restraints on charcoal production. This adversely affected the iron industry and its death knell began to sound when new techniques, using coking-coal, transferred the industry to the Severn gorge at Coalbrookdale in Shropshire. The Sussex landscape began to recover; water power previously utilised by the iron workers, was switched to the milling of corn. Many of those ponds have now been incorporated in the gardened estates of the nobility. The Ordnance Survey maps of the Weald are dotted with such names as 'forge-pond' and 'hammer-pond' - bearing witness to the former exploitation.

During all this time, Sussex was subjected to unwanted attention. The French attacked and burnt a number of towns and villages in 1377, and again in 1545. The former resulted in the raising of a new castle at Bodiam to protect the eastern flank, and the addition of defensive walls elsewhere. It was reported that the Rottingdean's church tower was set alight while the villagers were sheltering within it. In the same raid the Prior of Lewes, who marched to defend the coast, was captured and ransomed.

The 1545 raids saw attacks on Seaford and Brighton. Sir Nicholas Pelham's valiant action is commemorated on his memorial tablet in St. Michael's, Lewes, with the charming Tudor pun: 'What time the French sought to have sacked Seafoorde - This Pelham did repel 'em back aboard'. The raid on Brighton is graphically illustrated in a contemporary map showing the beached galleys of the invaders and bands of local militia coming towards Brighthelmstone to fight them off. The town is shown in flames, fanned by a sou'-westerly wind.

A Royal progress was equally unwelcome for the landowners whose costly duty it was to provide lodging and sustenance for the Sovereign and her entourage. Queen Elizabeth made a Royal progress in 1573, staying at Bridge, feasting under an oak at Northiam with fare provided by one Master Bishopp, dancing in the ornamental garden at Brickwall House (now a school for boys under the Frewen Educational Trust) and thence to Rye. On her visit to the ancient town, which she dubbed 'Rye Royal', she was presented with a purse of gold. Possibly her arrival was unexpected because the borough had to borrow the money from the Mayor. Her visit inspired one of Kipling's stories *Gloriana* in *Rewards and Fairies*. Later, in 1591, Lord Montagu welcomed the Queen and her nobles at Cowdray Park, Midhurst. Lavish entertainment of music and masque, shooting and angling, was matched only by the sumptuous excess of food. At breakfast on Monday 17th August three oxen and a hundred and forty geese were eaten. For the mistress of Cowdray, Lady Montagu, it was 'O joyfull daie'.

Between these two Elizabethan visits came a brush with potential disaster. The Sussex coast was alerted to the presence of the invading Spanish Armada when, on 19th July 1588, the warning beacons blazed along the coast. Philip of Spain intended to humiliate Protestant England by gaining control of the Channel before launching an invasion force from Flanders. An invasion scare two years earlier had shown how ill-prepared the undefended coast of Sussex was, and so, in 1587, the coast was surveyed and a map prepared which pointed to locations thought to be at most risk of invasion. A highly organised system of early warning beacons was put on alert.

By April of 1588, Thomas Sackville, Lord Buckhurst, in effective control of the county's defence because the Lord Lieutenant, Lord Howard of Effingham, nominally responsible, was away at sea in command of the fleet. Sackville realised that the required force of four thousand infantry, two

The Prince of Wales Feathers.

Tablet to Sir Nicholas Pelham.

King George IV.

John Fuller ('Mad Jack').

Lewes Castle.

Fuller's Pyramid Tomb.

Vandalised plaque at Battle.

Arundel Castle.

hundred and sixty cavalry and five ships had not been summoned and he remedied the defect. Even in those days the importance of communication was recognised, so, in addition to the beacon system, post-horses were to be kept in readiness all along the coast. The apprehension of the inhabitants can well be imagined for it was accepted that the Sussex coast was the most likely intended beach-head for the expected invasion. Anxious eyes, official watchers and the rest of the population would have kept a sharp lookout westward.

On July 25th the first sighting was made at Selsey, where a bridegroom, his best man and father-in-law - all members of the local defence force - took a short break to join the bride for the wedding itself before returning to duty. Sussex was not to be outdone by Drake's *sang-froid* at bowls! A rider set out and soon relays were spreading the news. One Spanish galleon, the *Carthagena*, was dismasted and beached at West Wittering. (A farmhouse nearby is named 'Carthagena' and tradition has it that timbers from the vessel were used in its construction.) On the same day, William Savage, the Vicar of Rottingdean, called his parishioners to the beach where they offered up devout prayers for deliverance. It seems their supplication was heeded for the Armada was harried by the English fleet all along the coast. The danger passed.

The Spanish fleet was near Beachy Head on 26th July and was becalmed off Fairlight on the 27th, before being able to cross to Calais. Fireships were sent in and during the ensuing panic the Spanish vessels scattered and were attacked by Drake, Hawkins and Frobisher. The once proud Armada was on the point of destruction when a change in wind allowed the remaining ships to escape into the North Sea.

The rest is history but, although Sussex rejoiced, there was much anti-Catholic revenge. The lifting of the danger encouraged some Puritans to give their children timely Christian names such as 'Bethankful' and 'Preserved'. The threat of invasion was rekindled by both Napoleon Bonaparte and Adolf Hitler in later centuries but, happily, front-line Sussex escaped yet again.

The following century brought more drama to the county when militant Puritanism came into conflict with the Crown. Towns, neighbours and even families had divided loyalties. Control of the county was important because the iron industry provided the tools of war from the Royal Foundries in St. Leonard's Forest. Support for Parliament was particularly strong among ordinary folk in the east whilst the gentry in the west were just as loyal to the throne.

Chichester, however, declared for the Roundheads in August 1642 but was under loyalist control only a month later. Cromwell's General, Sir William Waller, having taken Arundel, turned his attention to the now isolated cathedral city. Initial bombardment by inaccurate cannons did little damage but closer assault prevailed. The city surrendered and the religious fanatics in Waller's army desecrated the cathedral and its treasures.

In the winter of 1643, the King's General, Lord Hopton, made a surprise advance across a frozen county and retook Arundel and a number of other villages before Waller once again triumphed. The miseries of war encouraged many ordinary men of Sussex to support a 'stop the war' campaign and except for abortive Royalist risings in Horsham and Rye in 1648, the county played little part in the later stages of the Civil War. The conflict finally culminated in the trial and execution of Charles I, in January 1649, with the assent of seven of the county's notables.

During the period of Puritan supremacy the clergy were examined for any 'Popish practices' and the 'Triers' required them to write a statement of their beliefs. Dr. Aquila Cruso, Vicar of Sutton, outwitted them by writing in Greek and Hebrew, which none of the examiners could understand.

As a consequence of Charles II's escape after the Battle of Worcester in 1651, at which he tried to regain the throne, Sussex witnessed a very different royal progress. The King travelled under the alias of 'Will Jackson', a servant, his long hair having been cropped. It was impossible to disguise his height, however - a detail which a sharp-eyed Roundhead might have spotted.

The escape had the essence of high adventure. Crossing hostile territory, narrowly avoiding contact with some who might have recognised him and passing through pickets during the journey - all had elements of risk. That the King eventually reached Brighton bears witness to his own courage and the loyalty of friends who made the necessary arrangements. Some believe that he spent the last night in England at Ovingdean Grange, an idea developed in a novel of that name, by a popular Victorian author, Harrison Ainsworth. It is almost certain, however, that he was lodged at The George Inn in West Street, Brighton, where he was recognised by the landlord.

An introduction to Nicholas Tettersell, skipper of the coal brig *Surprise,* enabled him to leave Shoreham for France, at a price. At the restoration of the monarchy in 1660, Tettersell pressed his part in the adventure. He was handsomely rewarded, given a naval commission and renamed his boat *The Royal Escape.* Although not a popular figure among his fellow citizens, his tombstone - still to be seen in the churchyard of St. Nicholas in Brighton - bears an epitaph eulogising his achievement. In fact, the text had probably been written by Tetersell himself! An annual yacht race between Brighton and Fecamp commemorates the voyage.

Towards the end of the century, in 1690, another sea battle was witnessed from the cliff-top vantage point of Beachy Head. This time, however, it was the combined English and Dutch fleet that suffered a humiliating defeat at the guns of an eighty-strong force under the command of the Frenchman, Admiral Tourville. Arthur Herbert, Earl of Torrington, was ordered to attack the larger squadron by William III but, whilst the Dutch part of his command complied, Torrington retreated, only to be court-martialled for failing to engage. Although acquitted, he was not given another command. A very different sort of battle was waged in the skies above Beachy Head two hundred and fifty years later.

If Charles II's visit to Brighton was brief, a later sovereign was to enjoy a much extended association with the town. By the time George, Prince of Wales, arrived for his first stay in 1783, Brighthelmstone, as it was then called, had already benefited from the attraction of its sea water - with its restorative properties - for some thirty years. A book entitled *A Dissertation on the use of Sea-Water in the Diseases of the Glands* was published in 1750 by Richard Russell. Patients were advised to drink the water, suitably flavoured to make it palatable and, also to be dipped in the briny. So fashionable had this become - at a time when fashion was all important - that the resort began to overshadow the traditional fishing village. Fisher-folk recognised new ways of making a living by setting up as bathing attendants and by providing lodgings.

The Prince so enjoyed his holiday with his Uncle, the Duke of Cumberland, because of the many raffish distractions allowed, that he resolved to find a house for himself. That house, originally a farmhouse on the eastern edge of the town, was eventually transformed by John Nash into one of the most exotic buildings in the realm - The Royal Pavilion. The Prince's excesses were legendary, his lifestyle bizarre, and his tastes unusual, but they combined to create a glittering court housed in a building of cupolas and domes, friezes and fancies, decorated sumptuously with imported Chinese hangings, wallpapers, vases and ornaments.

As Prince of Wales, as the Prince Regent, and eventually as His Majesty King George IV, he never did things by halves. Illegally, as far as the Crown was concerned, he contracted a marriage, in 1785, with the most charming, but widowed, Roman Catholic, Maria Fitzherbert. It could never be sanctioned officially and she kept house a few yards away. It has been revealed, recently, that they produced two girls and five boys - an altogether intriguing tale. His official marriage to Princess Caroline of Brunswick, which took place a decade later, ended rapidly in great unhappiness. Their only child was the flamboyant Princess Charlotte. She was despatched to Worthing to cool her ardour for Captain Hesse of the 18th Hussars. Her eventual marriage to Prince Leopold Saxe-Coburg-Saarfeld in 1816 was also short-lived, her life ending tragically in childbirth the following year. The lack of an official heir to Prince George's daughter opened the way, eventually, for the accession of Victoria.

High society was naturally attracted to so glamorous a court, among them not a few rogues and charlatans, many of whom became part of the Prince's set. They included Lord Barrymore and his equally disreputable brothers, members of the Hellfire Club, and his sister. The quartet were dubbed respectively, 'Hellgate', 'Newgate', 'Cripplegate', and 'Billingsgate'. Hell would be his Lordship's inevitable destination; Newgate was the only prison the Rev. Augustus had not been in, whilst the

Hon. Henry was club-footed. Their sister possessed the picturesque vocabulary of a fishwife. Sir John Lade, the Prince's stable-master, and his wife, Letty, a hard-riding, hard-swearing former mistress of a notorious highwayman known as 'Sixteen-string Jack', were other accomplices, as was Captain George Hanger, an uncouth lover of the bottle with a penchant for duelling.

Their escapades were seized upon with glee by the caricaturists of the day who also turned their attention to the succession of rival mistresses taken up by the Prince - sundry beauties as well as the fascinating Lady Jersey, Lady Hertford and the ample Lady Conyngham.

In his defence, it must be said that his affection for Maria Fitzherbert continued, intermittently, for much of his life and at the King's death, the Duke of Wellington observed that her portrait was in a locket around his neck. In spite of his wildness the Prince was talented in music and the arts, and as a young man he was an accomplished horseman and whip. His more thoughtful friends, included Edmund Burke, Charles James Fox and Richard Brinsley Sheridan.

Momentous events of the European stage took place during the high season of the court at Brighton. Relatives and friends escaping the horrors of the French Revolution were entertained, having made the crossing direct from Dieppe; the local paper, *The Sussex Weekly Advertiser*, reported arrivals assiduously. One, the Duchess de Noailles was taken to watch a cricket match on the open space known as The Level. During the interval she enjoyed lunch in the marquee and listened to the Prince's band of music. Whether she enjoyed the cricket is debatable but the crowd enjoyed watching her as she strolled around the ground with Mrs Fitzherbert, for the paper records that her 'figure and deportment are remarkably interesting'.

In the following year, 1793, war with France meant that the army encamped nearby and the Prince was able to play the part of a warrior at the head of his troops. 'Brighton Camp' was immortalised in song, on canvas and on the pages of Miss Austen's *Pride and Prejudice*.

The town was for some years very much at the centre of affairs. Stage coaches, which had originally arrived via the county town of Lewes, soon came direct to Castle Square to speed the connection with the capital. But, inevitably, the era of importance passed. Although George IV's successor, his brother William IV, enjoyed Brighton and stayed there yearly throughout his reign, the link was broken by the disdain with which Queen Victoria held the town and its people.

Her preference for Osborne House on the Isle of Wight denuded the Pavilion of service - and of furniture - and eventually, after extraordinary local squabbles, the Pavilion was bought by the town. Despite damage by fire and hurricane the restoration of the Pavilion and its gardens has been achieved and is greatly admired by visitors from across the world. So dramatic a story as that of Prince, Regent and King, and his turbulent associations is naturally well documented. A list of books about his life and works is to be found in the bibliography.

Mass Dial on Bishopstone Church

The Sugar Loaf, Woods Corner

A restored Forge Pond, Sheffield Park

The Royal Pavilion, Brighton

The Norman castle built within
the walls of Roman Anderita.

The waterside at Bosham.

The Field of Hastings.

Lewes.

One of the major occupations in coastal counties, and particularly in Sussex, from the late seventeenth to the middle of the nineteenth century was that of smuggling. During that time the running of contraband cargoes was a major crime conducted on an enormous scale. It is difficult for us to realise how widespread and well-organised it was. A variety of goods had duties imposed on them and it was worth taking considerable risks in order to supplement meagre wages.

Ever since the first tax had been imposed in 1275, by Edward I, on fleeces sent to the continent, their illegal export had been the province of 'owlers' who ran cargoes across the Channel to meet the demand of the continental cloth industry. Edward's reason for levying a duty was an attempt to protect the home industry which was jeopardised by the loss of so much high quality wool. It was not until several centuries later that the illegal trade expanded into the more notorious import of a wide selection of goods.

Almost everything brought into the country was subject to duty and fortunes could be made by bringing these goods in illegally. Wine and spirits, tea and coffee, tobacco and spices, glass and china, silk and lace were all eagerly sought. Liquid cargoes were carried in casks holding almost four gallons, and dry items, in specially made oilskin coverings. Luggers were designed and built with secret storage space, and these vessels put into continental ports where the goods were readily available. Considerable outlay was needed for the purchase and much of this money was supplied by wealthy landowners who remained skilfully in the background whilst the actual risky operation was carried out by ordinary seamen and farm labourers.

Sussex was ideally placed to take advantage of the trade. The coastline was scarcely populated and the sea-crossing short. Seamen were skilled and knew, as well as the vagaries of wind and tide, where best their contraband could be landed. The operations would normally be undertaken on moonless nights. Gangs would be ready to unload the cargoes quickly and quietly and transport them in stages across the Weald towards the lucrative London markets.

Each operation was highly organised, from the financing of the cargoes and the choice of beach (with alternatives) for unloading, to the means of inland transport. The winding creeks of the Bosham area and the long, low sandy coastline from the Manhood Peninsula to Shoreham provided ideal landing sites, as did the wetlands around Pevensey and Rye. Cliffs presented no problems, for the gangs were able to derrick contraband from the beach below. Large scale operations also allowed for physical protection of the tubmen by well-armed batmen against a surprise challenge by customs officers. Ingenious signalling methods from the set of windmill sweeps and the playing of particular posthorn tunes, to lights in chosen windows and the use of signal 'spout' lanterns transmitted information about the advisability of the run. Deception and distraction often helped to outwit the endeavours of the preventive men.

Once unshipped, the cargoes were carried by men, ponies or carts to the hiding places. Churches and graveyards, derelict castles and barns, secret rooms and even ponds all provided hiding places *en route*. Relatively few of the cargoes landed were ever intercepted. Villages like Mayfield and Groombridge, Rottingdean and Alfriston, Jevington and East Dean could all command sizeable gangs ready at short notice to play their part. Most of the settlements engaged in the trade would be able to provide tunnels which linked capacious cellars.

In the eighteenth century the gangs might have numbered several hundred members, and in many cases they were prepared to resort to violence to ensure success. Farmers were coerced into co-operation and magistrates were often unwilling to convict those caught because of threats to themselves and their families.

Although whole communities would be happy to avail themselves of reasonably priced luxuries, the bulk of the trade was far removed from the cosy image of smuggling conveyed in Kipling's poem *A Smuggler's Song*. The guile, ingenuity, nerve and daring shown by many of the brotherhood has ensured that tales of their exploits have been passed down through generations, mostly embellished, but with sufficient detail to earn a grudging admiration. The long history of smuggling in Sussex has much fascination and is well presented in Mary Waugh's *Smuggling in Kent & Sussex 1700-1840* and in Hufton and Baird's *Scarecrows Legion*.

Until relatively recently the towns and villages of Sussex were precluded from much contact with London because the heavy clays of the Weald were an effective barrier - thick, sticky mud in winter and hard, rutted, axle-breaking rock in summer. Such was the nature of the clay that only two hundred and fifty years ago a learned physician claimed that Sussex girls had such shapely calves and ankles because they were forever pulling of their feet from the morass! For much of the winter only oxen had the strength to pull carts and coaches through the clay.

Until those conditions were improved, the county remained much as it had been for centuries - a peaceful agricultural backwater, with difficulty of access. Although with a 1663 Act of Parliament it became possible for Turnpike Trusts to be set up, the benefit did not affect most of Sussex until a century later. Trusts, often a good investment, were allowed to install toll barriers, and the charges collected were intended for maintaining the highway. The third quarter of the eighteenth century saw a rapid expansion of the system with substantial reductions in journey times, particularly of the stage-coaches, and regular schedules were introduced. London to Brighton was initially accomplished, in the 1790's, in about eight hours, but even this was brought down to five or six hours within thirty years. The number of services increased dramatically with the result that the resorts and the towns along the routes benefited considerably.

The colourful heyday of the coaching era, nostalgically recorded on prints, must have presented stirring sights and sounds for the sophisticated traveller and rustic admirer alike. A cavalcade indeed! The possibility of an encounter with a notorious highwayman added to the excitement posed by everyday hazards of reckless driving and overturned coaches.

Although commerce also took advantage of improved roads, bulky loads were still difficult to move, and so an alternative means of transport was sought for timber, coal, lime, wine and groceries. The peak of 'canal mania' followed that equal, but earlier enthusiasm for turnpikes. Navigations, based on existing rivers, and canal extensions were developed and maintained. The Arun-Wey Navigation allowed barge traffic to link the Thames with the coast at Littlehampton, and an offshoot led both to warehouses at a basin in Chichester and to the harbour at Portsmouth.

Progress was more sedate than on the frenetic highways but, nevertheless, loading and unloading of barges at wharves and the chance of refreshment at inns added a focus for the rural population. Sturdy horses worked with the narrow boats from the tow-path, although where tunnels were used, as at Hardham, the bargees had to propel the boat by lying on the deck and using leg power against the walls. Great landowners were usually involved in the developments - Lord Sheffield, with the Upper Ouse Navigation and Lord Egremont, with the Rother. But they and more lowly shareholders could hardly have foreseen the coming of the iron-road which was to provide serious and even terminal opposition.

Whilst the turnpikes could carry passengers and the canals, the products of commerce, the railways could do both! From the 1840's the rail network spread from the focus of the capital. The 'navvies' who had been brought in to dig the Navigation Canals now turned their energies to the monumental task of digging cuttings, building embankments and driving tunnels. Architects' dreams were realised with the creation of such wonders as the Balcombe viaduct and the Italianate station facade at Brighton.

The steam era introduced puffing, clanking, screeching engines and carriages to a hitherto peaceful countryside. Although not without danger, (accidents did happen), steam trains had a glamour which is still attractive. They also transported ever increasing numbers from London for relaxation and recreation, to Down and Weald, coast and river. More and more people could enjoy the beauty of the countryside and even return the same day to the burgeoning suburbs; the railway also introduced a new phenomenon - the commuter. Sussex could never be the same again. Grafted onto this pattern was superimposed the freedom given by the motor car, and yet, fortunately, there are still parts of the landscape which evoke the tranquillity of the past.

The great and the good still came to Sussex and so, too, did thousands of their countrymen. Royal progresses continued, but with much less fanfare than in the days of Elizabeth I and George IV. 137

Edward, as Prince of Wales and as King, would come to Brighton to stay with his daughter, the Duchess of Fife. King George V's association with Sussex was through periods of convalescence at Craigwell House, Aldwick, and, as a result, Bognor was dignified with the suffix 'Regis'. He also stayed at Eastbourne and was a guest of John Christie at Glyndebourne, near Lewes. It was here, under the shadow of the isolated dome of The Caburn, in the grounds of his lovely house, that Christie created an opera house, whose productions became legend in the world of music. Exactly sixty years after the first night of the original house, which opened with *Le nozze di Figaro* the same overture burst into life in a new, and even more beautiful auditorium created by the founder's son, Sir George Christie.

Music has not been inspired as much as literature by the magic of the Sussex countryside, but several compositions are most worthy of mention. Sir Edward Elgar and his wife lived declining years in a cottage called Brinkwells, near Fittleworth and it was here that he composed the haunting cello concerto as a tribute to all those who lost their lives in the Great War. It contrasts in mood with the violin concerto created just nine years earlier which reflects the buoyant enthusiasm and confidence of an empire at its most successful.

Fittingly, Sir Hubert Parry set to music Blake's preface to *Milton* - the composition being known as *Jerusalem* - whilst living at Rustington, close to Felpham where the poet himself had written his famous text. Blake had been thinking of the Downs when he wrote: 'And did those feet in ancient time/ Walk upon England's mountains green?' Fortunately the great anthem is still kept alive being sung at the start of many meetings of the Women's Institute. *Sussex by the Sea* was written in the same locality at South Berstead by William Ward Higgs.

And so the Cavalcade passes. Made up of Kings and Queens, Lords and Ladies, but mainly by ordinary and extraordinary men and women, it will continue to do so. We cannot possibly know what the future holds in store, but certainly Sussex will be as lovely, as stimulating and as creative in the coming centuries as it has been in the past. The most that we can do is to try to ensure that its glories are not forgotten and that we pass to our children's children a heritage as little sullied as possible.

SELECT BIBLIOGRAPHY

Books relating to each chapter.

I	Lucas, E. V.	*Highways and Byways in Sussex*	Macmillan	1904
	Martin, C. & Parker, G.	*The Spanish Armada*	Hamish Hamilton	1988
II	Blunden, E.	*Shelley*	O.U.P.	1965
	Churchill, W. S.	*My Early Life*	Macmillan	1930
	Grylls, R. G.	*Trelawny*	Constable	1950
	Leslie, A.	*Mr Frewen of England*	Hutchinson	1966
III	Janney, S.	*Life of William Penn*	Philadelphia Friends	1882
IV	Kingsford, P. W.	*F. W. Lanchester*		
	Kipling, R.	*Fox-Hunting from The Muse among the Motors*		1904
	Straker, E.	*Wealden Iron*	Bell	1931
	Thirkell, A.	*Three Houses*	O.U.P.	1931
	Volk, C.	*Magnus Volk of Brighton*	Phillimore	1971
V	de Selincourt, H.	*The Cricket Match*		
	Macdonell, A. G.	*England their England*	Macmillan	1951
	Moens, S. M.	*Rottingdean - The story of a Village*	Beal	1952
VI	Belloc, H.	*The Four Men*	Nelson	1912
	Benson, E. F.	*Miss Mapp*	Hutchinson	1922
	Bogarde, D.	*A Postillion Struck by Lightning*	Chatto & Windus	1977
	Bogarde, D.	*Great Meadow - An Evocation*	Viking	1992
	Carrington, C.	*Rudyard Kipling*	Macmillan	1955
	Cohen, M.	*Rudyard Kipling to Rider Haggard*	Hutchinson	1965
	Copper, Bob	*A Song for Every Season*	Heinemann	1971
	Copper, Bob	*Songs and Southern Breezes*	Heinemann	1973
	Copper, Bob	*Early to Rise*	Heinemann	1976
	Copper, Bob	*Across Sussex with Belloc*	Alan Sutton	1994
	Edwardes, T.	*Neighbourhood*	Methuen	1911
	Edwardes, T.	*Tansy*	Palmer	1921
	Fairless, M.	*The Roadmender*	Duckworth	1913
	Hopkins, R. T.	*Sheila Kaye-Smith*	Palmer	1925
	Hudson, W. H.	*Nature in Downland*	Longmans	1906

	Jefferies,R.	*Nature Near London*	Chatto & Windus	1941
	Kaye-Smith, S.	*The Tramping Methodist*	Cassell	1908
	Kaye-Smith, S.	*Green Apple Harvest*	Cassell	1920
	Kaye-Smith, S.	*Joanna Godden*	Cassell	1921
	Kipling, R.	*Puck of Pook's Hill*	Macmillan	1906
	Kipling, R.	*Rewards and Fairies*	Macmillan	1910
	Kipling, R.	*Sussex* (poem from *The Five Nations*)	Macmillan	1903
	Kipling, R.	*They (Traffics and Discoveries)*	Macmillan	1904
	Kipling, R.	*Something of Myself*	Macmillan	1937
	Millgate, M.	*Thomas Hardy*	O.U.P.	1987
	Palmer, G. & Lloyd, N.	*E. F. Benson as he was*	Lennard	1988
	Payne, S. (Ed)	*Barclay Wills' 'The Downland Shepherds'*	Alan Sutton	1989
	Reavell, C. & T.	*E. F. Benson*	Martello	1984
	Smith, M.	*Rudyard Kipling - the Rottingdean Years*	Brownleaf	1989
	Wilson, A. N.	*Hilaire Belloc*	Hamilton	1987
VII	Longford, E.	*Pilgrimage of Passion*		
	Strachey, L.	*Eminent Victorians*	Chatto	1918
VIII	Ham, J.	*Storrington in Georgian & Victorian Times*		
	Kilvert, R. F.	*Diary: 1870-1879 (3 Vols)*		1938-40
	Scott, H.	*Secret Sussex*	Batchworth	1949
	Wagner, A. & Dale, A.	*The Wagners of Brighton*	Phillimore	1983
	Smith, M.	*The Grange*	Rottingdean Preservation Soc	1993
IX	Morley, Lord	*Life of Richard Cobden (2 Vols)*	Chapman Hall	1881
	Stephen, Lady	*Emily Davies and Girton*	Constable	1927
	Willard, B.	*Sussex*	Batsford	1965
X	Ainsworth, H.	*Ovingdean Grange*	Routledge	undated
	Austen, J.	*Pride and Prejudice*	O.U.P.	1813
	Beamish, T.	*Battle Royal*	Muller	1965
	Bryant, R.	*Warriors of the Dragon Gold*	Mildmay	1987
	Foord-Kelsey, J. & P.	*Mrs Fitzherbert and Sons*	The Book Guild	1991
	Harper, C. G.	*The Brighton Road*	Chatto & Windus	1892
	Hibbert, C.	*George IV - Prince of Wales*	Longmans	1972
	Howarth, D.	*1066 - The Year of the Conquest*	Viking	1978

Hufton, G. & Baird, E.	*Scarecrows Legion*	Rochester	1983
Margary, I.	*Roman Ways in the Weald*	Phoenix Hse	1948
Morris, J.	*Domesday Book - Sussex*	Phillimore	1976
Musgrave, C.	*Life in Brighton*	Hallewell	1970
Savage, A. (Ed)	*The Anglo-Saxon Chronicles*	Heinemann	1982
Sitwell, O. & Barton, M.	*Brighton*	Faber	1935
Vine, P. A. L.	*London's Lost Route to the Sea*	David & Charles	1965
Wardroper, J.	*The Caricatures of George Cruikshank*	Gordon Fraser	1977
Waugh, M.	*Smuggling in Kent & Sussex 1700-1840*	Countryside	1985
Wilson, D. M.	*The Bayeux Tapestry*	Thames & Hudson	1985

INDEX